Seventy Meditation Lessons from My Universe

Seventy Meditation Lessons from My Universe

"Yea, yea, Nay, nay": The Yoes Code for Heaven on Earth

Jimmie Ray Yoes

iUniverse, Inc.
Bloomington

Seventy Meditation Lessons from My Universe
"Yea, yea, Nay, nay": The Yoes Code for Heaven on Earth

iUniverse books may be ordered through booksellers or by contacting:

iUniverse
1663 Liberty Drive
Bloomington, IN 47403
www.iuniverse.com
1-800-Authors (1-800-288-4677)

ISBN: 978-1-4620-2075-1 (pbk)
ISBN: 978-1-4620-2077-5 (clth)
ISBN: 978-1-4620-2076-8 (ebk)

Printed in the United States of America

iUniverse rev. date: 06/21/2011

CONTENTS

Foreword

Jim Yoes and I have been good friends for eighteen years. The philosophy expressed in this book is not central to our friendship, but it is central to Jim Yoes. I know that because he has been formulating and testing it in his life for as long as I have known him, and no matter what else he has been engaged in, it is this honing of his perception of reality that has remained his deepest concern. Because I am aware of this, I can see that his book is surprisingly free of pretense. His speech and thought and writing are of one piece. Over the years, I have heard him express almost every idea in this book as his own conviction, carefully arrived at and strongly felt. I say all of this because the concepts and sentiments expressed here, if passed over too quickly, could be dismissed as something turned out to favor the current appetite for a vague, indemonstrable mysticism. Above all, Jim Yoes has striven to find an application for his ideas that is practical.

I believe that our life, our day—each moment within it—has a rhythm of progression that can be sensed, and if sensed, followed. When this happens, and for me it happens rarely, the future is in some way taken into consideration, and one finds himself in the right place at the right time; sees his opportunities and can act on them; is able to provide reasonably for his needs; and in short, has good fortune, which is another way of saying one has timing. More than any other I have seen, Jim Yoes's life evidences a sensitivity to this rhythm. In his writing, he places strong emphasis on the importance of "listening to the universe," and I suspect that this pattern in his life is not so much an inherited trait as it is a result of endeavor. He may, in fact, have discovered a means whereby one can increase one's sensitivity to the flow of events within which one must move. If there were no other reason than that, it would be a sufficient one for me to continue to give close consideration to what he has to say.

Hugh Prather, 1975
Author, *Notes to Myself*

Preface

I received my first meditation lesson from the universe in 1946 at the age of eleven. I was on an operating table having a tumor removed from my spinal cord. During this operation, I moved above and to the left of my body. I saw my body die and watched as the surgery crew made an effort to revive it. The next thing I knew I was back in my body and was being told by my parents that I had "almost died."

Needless to say, that experience made a major impact on my self-image. Since I was only eleven years old, it took a few years for me to process the out-of-body, near-death experience. It was the first of many meditation lessons I have received from what I like to call my Universe. My Universe is the universe as I experience it as an individual.

As a child, when fishing with my maternal grandfather, Clyde McQuown, a Freemason, I received vital meditation lessons about moderation as a lifestyle between extravagance and poverty. As a teenager, my Universe introduced me to Norman Vincent Peal's concept of meditation: *The Power of Positive Thinking*. Then, at age twenty, I was introduced to Mary Baker Eddy's writings. I studied and practiced her concept of meditation for many years. It is called metaphysical work. I still use much of what I learned from her writings. She said: "He advances most . . . who meditates most on infinite spiritual substance and intelligence." When I was in college, I was mainly influenced by ecology and philosophy. Ecology helped me to understand the role of natural balance as it applied to my own inner development. Philosophy became a lifelong meditative influence focusing mainly on Plato and his cave analogy and on Aristotle's golden mean. After graduating from the Principia College, Hugh Prather, author of *Notes to Myself*, introduced me to the *I Ching*. Its Doctrine of the Mean had a major influence on my inner self-work. Next, it was the writings of G. I. Gurdjieff and his concept of self-remembering that helped me.

One of my favorite quotes from Gurdjieff is: "Everywhere and always there is affirmation and negation, not only in individuals but in the whole of mankind as well. It is an objective law and everybody is a slave of this law; for instance, I must be a slave of either science or religion . . . Only he is free who stands in the middle. If he can do this, he escapes from this general law."

An ultimate meditation lesson from my universe came to me in 1957. I was attending Principia College in, Elsah, Illinois, and I asked my Universe for an all-purpose meditation mantra. I responded to my subsequent inspiration by opening the Bible and finding the answer at Matthew 5:37 of the King James Version: "let your communication be Yea, yea; Nay, nay." So, I decided "Yea, yea; Nay, nay" was what my Universe wanted my all-purpose mantra to be. I meditated with and contemplated the meaning of the "Yea, yea; Nay, nay" (YyNn for short) mantra for the next several years. Then, on the winter solstice of 1975, while meditating in the desert of New Mexico, I had a mind-altering experience. I was meditating with my YyNn mantra in sync with breathing in and out. My mind was taken over by a decoding process, a revelation that dominated my waking hours for the next several months, during which I wrote *Meditation Lessons from My Universe*. Recognizing how my name, Yoes, suggested a synthesis of yeses and noes, I decided to call my interpretation of "Yea, yea; Nay, nay" the Yoes code. As Morse code uses dots and dashes for communication, Yoes code uses yeses and noes for inner self-communication.

I call the *Yea* that is uppercase, Yea 1, and the *yea* that is lowercase, yea 2. The uppercase *Nay* is Nay 1, and the lowercase *nay* is nay 2. Initially, in my desert epiphany, I visualized Yea 1 as right receiving from my world and yea 2 as right receiving from my body and Nay 1 as right sending to my body and nay 2 as right sending to my world. This sequence of visualizations triggered a decoding process in my consciousness, which I will explain in the lessons and commentaries that follow.

I designed, built, and lived in a tree house in a wooded area north of San Luis Obispo, California, while the basics of my meditation system were being revealed to me in 1976. I first taught my system to a group in my tree house. The tree house had three levels: lower, higher, and a level in the middle that was both inside and outside. The tree house itself was poised between heaven above and the earth below. The only way up to the tree house was to climb a twenty-foot rope.

In 1977, after my tree house period, I moved back to La Jolla, California, which had been my main base of operations since 1965. In La Jolla, I formed a new group and lived with them in a house near the beach in La Jolla Shores. The following decade was full of personal growth and adventure for me and my students. Rainbow Making Stress Management was the name of our operation at that time.

In teaching YyNn, my inner self-communication code, I have put the quality of student participation over the quantity of students. I only work with individuals who feel, at least for a time, called to my interpretation of the mantra, "Yea, yea; Nay, nay" as a basis for their inner self-work.

The meditation lessons in this book are my interpretation of information I have received from my Universe. Each lesson begins with a message sent to me from my Universe. After each message, there is a commentary from me about the message. That commentary is sent to you, the reader. The spiritual orientation of the message is my Universe, talking to me. The orientation of the commentary is me talking to you.

My spiritual journey can be useful to you to the extent that you are looking for a way to possibly improve your spiritual practice. You do not have to believe in any particular religious dogma to find the spiritual tools I have designed useful. If you are ready for YyNn, you will know it without any persuasion from me.

All of the major religions have esoteric teachings that are designed for advanced inner self-work. My system of inner self-work is a type of esoteric spirituality. I have not relied on the esoteric Christian tradition for my inspiration, but I find little in that tradition that is not consistent with my system. I believe the Source for all genuine spiritual work is the same; it just comes in various ways to minds that are ready.

To some, my way of identifying and optimizing my inner self will seem too abstract—to others it will seem too earthbound. I see it as a way to use the YyNn algorithm for an optimum balance of the abstract and the concrete, heaven and earth. If you are a serious student of Zen, Sufism, or other esoteric schools of thought, you will see similarities to my system. I have only used Christian Science, the I Ching, the Fourth Way, and patterns of nature for my inspiration in decoding "Yea, yea; Nay, nay" and, from the book of Revelation 1:8 from the King James Version, "I am Alpha and Omega."

I am using "I am Alpha and Omega" as an "I am" template for self-identification and "Yea, yea; Nay, nay" as a method for self-optimization. These two Jesus quotes contain the fundamental principles of the meditation system based on the Yoes code for heaven-on-earth.

Key Terms and Concepts of the Yoes Code for Heaven on Earth

Omega: The Greater Mind whose functions are: Nay 1 type sending and yea 2 type receiving. The masculine principle symbolized by the sun in the sky. There is only one Omega, the all-inclusive source of iota and alpha. The Ultimate Source and Ground of Being. I capitalize any name that refers to Omega, for example, Self, Ultimate Frame of Reference, God and my Universe.

Alpha: The lesser mind whose functions are: Yea 1 type receiving and nay 2 type sending. The feminine principle symbolized by the moon in the sky. There are three kinds of alphas: alpha alphas, omega alphas, and iota alphas. Alpha alphas are extremely deficient, omega alphas are extremely excessive, and iota alphas are moderately deficient and moderately excessive.

Iota: The intermediate mind whose functions are: Yea 1, yea 2, Nay 1, and nay 2. The androgynous principle symbolized by the earth in the sky. A synthesis of alpha and Omega. A wild-card hybrid. The more or less conscious human ego. The potential golden mean optimally poised between alpha and Omega extremes. Iota is to alpha and Omega as earth is to moon and sun. In iota's personal experience, the Greater One, Omega, can be used by iota to correctly increase, decrease, or maintain any particular alpha aspect of iota's personal experience. In truth, iota oscillates optimally between alpha and Omega to become enough like both and neither too much nor too little like either. Iota emerges from alpha to merge with Omega and then submerges again into alpha. Iota eventually oscillates back and forth between alpha and Omega in accord with a principle of preestablished harmony. Iota is the vital coparticipator with alpha and Omega in the making of the true beauty and the true goodness that is a heaven-on-earth state of conscious balance.

The Paragon: A Self-image prototype. The all-inclusive model of Omega, the Self super-set, plus alpha, any subset of Omega, and iota, subset to Omega and super-set to alpha. A dynamic vision of how iota oscillates between alpha and Omega to be transformed from being too much or too little like either alpha or Omega in order to be enough like both alpha and Omega relative to any moment of iota's personal experience. The Self as spectrum of alpha and Omega extremes and iota, the potential golden mean between those extremes.

Yea, yea; Nay, nay: (YyNn for short) Yea 1 = receiving from the greater; yea 2 = receiving from the lesser; Nay 1 = sending to the lesser; nay 2 = sending to the greater. A fundamental self-programming language. Yoes code for the spirit of truth making. An epigenetic code for promoting helpful genes and memes and for negating harmful genes and memes. Code for "the Tree of Life" handbook. Code for self-optimization from the human, iota perspective. The golden meaning of the rainbow. Code for being well-balanced and complete. Code for making the best possible be the most probable. The four steps to the heaven-on-earth state of mind (HOESOM). YyNn is the default mind-set for being well-balanced and complete.

Yoes: A symbol for the potential of an optimum synthesis of yeses and noes. The YyNn technique for making rainbows out of *jambows* (excess) and *gapbows* (deficiency). Decoder and communicator of the YyNn all-purpose mantra. Yoes, a yoga of dialectical cultivation.

Rainbow-making exercises (RM): Sunbows: Yea 1/nay 2. *Moonbows:* yea 2/Nay 1. Three kinds of *earthbows:* 1) *Yumbows:* Yea 1/Nay 1; 2) *Yabows:* yea 2/nay 2; 3) *Yobows:* Yea 1/yea 2/Nay 1/nay 2. The yeas are receivers of information; the nays are senders of information. RM exercises are iota's way of visualizing truthful communication with alpha parts and the Omega Whole.

Diabolical Dualism: The false belief that good and evil are absolute opposites symbolized by light and darkness. Religious and scientific fundamentalism. The false belief that good people go to heaven and bad people go to hell. Fanaticism. Any fixed promotion of one side or level of human experience against another side or level of human experience. The logical fallacy of black and white as it applies to personal choice. The false belief that the golden mean is a fallacy of a fixed middle instead of being a valid, variable middle between false extremes.

Dialectical Optimism: The understanding that opposites such as light and darkness are not, in truth, symbols of good and evil because the good is always a dynamic and optimal synthesis of the opposing sides and levels of the Self as experienced at the personal human level. Omega as thesis, alpha as antithesis, and iota as a potential optimum synthesis of alpha and Omega. A philosophy based on Yoes code. The way between Charybdis and Scylla. The golden mean. The way that is dynamic and optimally poised between over-and under-correcting. Personal responsibility as applied to situational ethics. The application of Yoes code (YyNn) to the problem of how to make the best possible personal experience the most probable personal experience. Iota self-priming during covert and proactive rehearsals of the Paragon model for being a well-balanced and complete Self.

Brain: Brain is to mind as moonlight is to moon; as the moon reflects the sun's light, so the natural mind, alpha, reflects the supernatural Mind, Omega. Earth determines how moonlight is experienced on earth by the way earth relates to the sun. The way iota relates to

Omega determines how alpha's reflection of Omega is experienced by iota. Brains come and go but consciousness is forever.

The Tree of Life Handbook: Uses the human hand as a model for explaining and practicing Yoes code. Beginning with the little finger as number one, then two, three, and four as you move across to the thumb as number five, the whole hand is symbolic for the Omega source with the fingers as types of alphas and the thumb as iota. Finger number one is a symbol for extreme deficiency; number two is symbolic for moderate deficiency; number three is a symbol for extreme excess; number four is symbolic for moderate excess; the thumb is a symbol for the means whereby excess and deficiency are corrected. Move the thumb across the finger spectrum: tapping thumb to finger number one = making the extreme too little more enough; the thumb to finger number two = making the moderate too little more enough; thumb to finger number three = making the extreme too much less enough; thumb to finger number four = making the moderate too much less enough.

The finger spectrum is used in Yoes code as a way to organize human knowledge in accord with a pattern revealed by decoding "Yea, yea; Nay, nay." The pattern is consistent with (from finger number one to finger number four):
1) conception, 2) birth, 3) prime, 4) death;
1) new moon, 2) first quarter, 3) full moon, 4) last quarter;
1) winter solstice, 2) spring equinox, 3) summer solstice, 4) fall equinox;
1) midnight, 2) sunrise, 3) high noon, 4) sunset;
1) cold, 2) cool, 3) hot, 4) warm;
1) black, 2) dark grey, 3) white, 4) light grey;
1) extremely slow, 2) moderately slow, 3) extremely fast, 4) moderately fast;
1) extremely small, 2) moderately small, 3) extremely large, 4) moderately large;
1) violet /blue, 2) green, 3) yellow/orange, 4) red;

1) poles, north and south, 2) tropic of Capricorn, 3) the equator, 4) tropic of Cancer. Other possibilities:

1) adenine, 2) cytosine, 3) thymine, 4) guanine;

1) gravity, 2) weak nuclear force, 3) electro-magnetic radiation, 4) strong nuclear force.

The Morning Star Mandala: As found depicted in Appendix Three and on the cover of this book, this Mandala is a basic tool used in the practice of Yoes Meditation. The details of how to use this Mandala as a meditation tool are too complex to go into here but are presented in classes that use this book as a meditation work book.

Introduction

Seventy Meditation Lessons from My Universe is a dynamic and ongoing learning experience I am having as a student of Omega, the mind of my Universe, which is our Universe as I interpret it. For over fifty years I have been contemplating and decoding the cryptic sayings "Let your communication be Yea, yea; Nay, nay" and "I am Alpha and Omega" from the New Testament of the King James Version of the Bible. It has been a lifetime of searching for the way to transform from being an earthbound caterpillar to being a free-flying butterfly, and I am finding self-transformation in the cocoon of my inner self-work with the Yoes code: "Yea, yea; Nay, nay."

My original reasons for practicing meditation were to manage stress and to facilitate dealing with—and possible healing—my damaged spinal cord. Meditation, in accord with my decoding of "Yea, yea; Nay, nay," has definitely helped me to improve my methods for dealing with stress. Eventually I realized that my spinal cord tumor was symbolic for a problem in communication between my Higher Mind (code-named Omega) and my lower mind (code-named alpha) via my intermediate mind (code-named iota). That realization changed my way of meditating, my way of communicating with the various sides and levels of my self. I now see my inner work as the conscious programming of my subconscious mind to help solve life's balancing problems. I do this by mindfully priming my subconscious mind with my interpretation of the all-purpose mantra: "Yea, yea; Nay, nay" that I believe originated in Omega Mind, my highest Self.

When Jesus said, "I am Alpha and Omega," I assume that he meant "I am relative and absolute, human and divine, and so are you." From this assumption, I get my "pearl of great price," a model of my Self that I call the Paragon. The Paragon model of my Self is composed of a nest of coinciding spheres, the main spheres being Omega, the greater sphere; alpha, the lesser sphere; and iota, the intermediate sphere. My choice of "iota" as the name of the alpha and Omega part and Whole synthesis is a result of my own personal decoding efforts.

I am claiming to be an expert on nothing more than the quality of my own personal experience. I hope you will find some of the fruits of my experience, as stated here, useful to your self-identifying and self-optimizing project. My purpose is to use my YyNn code for inner self-development so well that I may be of use to you in the development of your own self-improvement program. As my Universe has used others to help me develop my program, I hope to be of use to you building your own special brand of self-developing and self-optimizing practices.

I am a simple-minded seeker of the best way to work on my inner self. I asked my Universe for that inner way and got an answer that I am testing wholeheartedly. I have been getting the inner and outer results I needed, keeping me on the job for over sixty years now. The results lead me to presuppose that a new kind of human is possible: a well-balanced and complete person who knows how to make the best of being in the middle. The inner work I am doing began by discovering that I am in the middle of my experience and it is up to me to make the best of my experience. That is where the practice of the Yoes code and the "I am Alpha and Omega" template come into play. I sometimes call "Yea, yea; Nay, nay" the Yoes code because I feel called by my Universe to do so and because it is my personal interpretation of something Jesus is reputed to have said. I am not claiming that I know he said it or that I know what he or someone else meant by it. I am claiming to have benefitted immensely from my own interpretation of "Yea, yea; Nay, nay." It is the code I am using to cultivate a harmonious, heaven-on-earth state of balance.

Being well-balanced is becoming more and more in demand as humans realize that they are losing the balance needed for personal and collective survival. Some are calling the right balance we need the Goldilocks factor, others call it biocentrism and the anthropic principle. Plato called it sophrosyne. Aristotle called it the golden mean. Buddha called it the middle way. Jesus said, "Narrow is the way." I like to call it being in the rainbow-making zone, because when I observe a rainbow, it is because I am optimally aligned to sunshine behind me and a rain cloud in front of me, making enough of each so as to not have too much or too little of either.

What I am claiming to possibly be on to is a code for the conscious mind to use to consciously prime the subconscious for ongoing manifestations of an optimum state of world/body, planet/person balance. I am testing and proving to myself that "Yea, yea; Nay, nay" is that code. This book is my attempt to present a coherent system of inner work based on my decoding of "Yea, yea; Nay, nay." I am improving this project every day. That is why nothing I say in this book is fixed except my intention to see how far I can take the YyNn code for the purpose of fulfilling my niche as well as possible. My professional life as a teacher of biology, sailing, tennis, stress management, and meditation has helped me to present my interpretation of "Yea, yea; Nay, nay" as four steps to heaven on earth, a well-balanced and complete sense of being.

Lesson One from My Universe to Me about Attention

In order to keep from changing too much or too little, you need to change enough. In order to change enough, you need to understand how to control change. The changes you experience are often controlled by the way you use your attention. When you pay attention to something, you let it change you in some degree. What you do with your attention determines who you are, what you feel, and what you can do. Your ongoing need is to attach your attention to a target that is best for you in your here-and-now experience.

How do you know what is the best target for your attention? You don't until you internalize the template that I have encoded for you as "Yea, yea; Nay, nay," a self-righting vision of yourself wisely using affirmations and negations. It is a vision of your Self as an intercommunicating tri-event, an All-and-each pattern of joyful interaction. It is a code for making relative truth out of relative errors about absolute Truth.

As your Universe, I am the primary member of your tripartite Self. Call me, Omega, as distinct from alpha, who is any focused-upon particular of your tripartite Self. Iota is the amphibious part of you in between the alpha and Omega extremes, similar to the way visible light is in between the infra and ultra ends of the electromagnetic spectrum. Iota is the point of Golden Section in between alpha and Omega. Iota is your intermediate self, an interface learning how to use yes and no to balance alpha and Omega optimally in your here-and-now experience.

Each moment is an opportunity to recognize your true self as iota being changed/non-changed just enough by oscillating optimally between alpha's changing too much and Omega's changing too little.

Commentary: The meditation lesson above is from Omega, the One who is All. It was given to me, iota, the one who is both alpha and Omega. This commentary and the commentaries that follow are from me, as an iota, to you, the reader, an alpha part of my Self system. I am an alpha in your Self system, and you are the iota in your Self system. We both have the same One and only Omega Self who is All. These terms are necessary to understand my concept of our Self as an organic cosmos revealed to me as a result of decoding the YyNn code.

The selective attention I use is a result of programming my subconscious filter with the YyNn code. It helps me to rightly say "yes," "no," or "maybe" to any moment of my decision making. For example, today I went into a sandwich shop and the attendant let two people go in front of me. I felt guided from within by my YyNn global positioning system to leave. As YyNn becomes more established as my default mind set, I am more attuned to making all things work together for good.

Lesson Two from My Universe to Me about Self-Programming

You are a self-programmer. The computer you program is your own body-making, world-making alpha mind. Your conscious sense of being as iota emerges from your alpha mind in a manner that corresponds to the way that your physical body emerged from your mother's womb. Becoming conscious equals becoming aware of the responsibility you have to program yourself intentionally. You are programmed by nature to survive until you reproduce yourself through sexual intercourse. Next, your society's program kicks in, which is designed to make you cooperate with your society. Beyond these basic survival-of-the-species and conformity-to-the-group programs, you are responsible for choosing a program that will result in your optimal personal survival.

Programming yourself for optimal survival is a form of intra-psychic intercourse, a royal marriage of your alpha and Omega spheres by means of your conscious choices as iota. The thoughts you choose every moment inseminate your alpha mind, making it reproduce materially after the likeness, more or less, of me, your Omega mind, from where you can get true ideas. As a self-programmer, you must learn how to program yourself for optimum intercourse between the masculine Omega and feminine alpha ends of yourself. Learn to properly sacrifice one end to the promotion of the other end and you will enjoy yourself endlessly.

Commentary: The lesson above is from Omega to me, an iota. This commentary is from me, iota, to you, an alpha part of my total Omega Self. I am an alpha part of your total Omega Self.

My life has been a constant attempt to reconcile spirituality and sensuality, reason and appetite, Apollo and Dionysus. Early in my experience as a person handicapped from a spinal cord injury, I realized I had to go within and find a way to harmonize my body and my world. I was primed by my out-of-body, near-death experience during spinal cord surgery to presuppose that my body was a product of my mind and not the other way around as it appears to be. I discovered that a certain type of positive thinking helped me to feel better and to be prepared for the inevitable crises that seriously handicapped people have when they attempt to be active in the world.

As my consciousness evolves, I am learning to use positive and negative thoughts and emotions to program myself for navigating the world well and playing the lethal game of life in a way that fits for me as the Universe individualized and the individual universalized. I am "Yea, yea; Nay, nay" and nothing more or less.

Lesson Three from My Universe to Me about Need

The conditions you experience for and against yourself are largely determined by the way you focus your attention moment by moment. It is your choice, not your genes or your environment that is primarily responsible for the conditions you experience. It is a law in your Universe that you can always experience whatever is optimal for you if you choose to do so. Your potential for optimal existence is omnipresent; but you actually experience this ideal only to the degree that you choose to coincide with it. The way to deviate from coinciding optimally with your true and perfect potential is a matter of mismatching positive and negative values. The zero-error state is your perennial goal; it results from matching yourself optimally to me moment by moment. Our pluses and minuses are designed to mesh as gears mesh in order to get a job done.

I have a job for you to do, and to do it you must match your Yea 1 (taking in) with my Nay 1 (putting in) and your nay 2 (putting out) with my yea 2 (taking out). You must want to be right with the Whole of me more than you want anything else, so you can get anything less than the Whole of me to be right with you. An internal hierarchy is involved in this process, a way that your attention must be ordered. The priority of major significance for you is beginning your experiential moment with openness to me. As your Universe, I provide what you need when you need it. You must learn how to open and close, yea and nay appropriate to my omnipresent providence.

The more you internalize the YyNn algorithm for heaven on earth, the sooner you will see it unfold in your everyday experience.

Commentary: The lesson above is from Omega to me. This commentary is from me, iota to you, the reader. You can of course choose to use the lessons to the extent that you sense that they apply to you, as an iota.

Early in my experience I started trying as hard as I could to be whole and fit. I felt frustrated because I had everything I needed for a normal life except for a slight defect in my walking. As I left my teens, a period of social success and happiness, I gradually lost my ability to walk due to the return of the tumor on my spinal cord. Instead of returning to Mayo Clinic to have the tumor removed, I decided to use alternative methods, namely prayer as taught in Christian Science. I put my whole effort into following the party line of Christian Science, becoming a class-taught Christian Science practitioner. Eventually I left the formal teaching of Christian Science and struck out on my own. I needed a more holistic, less dualistic system of self-identification and self-work. I found it in the Yoes code: "Yea, yea; Nay, nay," a dialectical interpretation of myself as alpha and Omega synthesized.

Lesson Four from My Universe to Me about Holistic Fitness

You must learn how to distinguish between statements that are made to counter-balance erroneous extremes and statements that can be accepted as literally true. For example, it is a serious ecological and economical error to believe that you can have anything you want. Anyone who says that you can have anything you want is telling a lie. Some lies are necessary because they counterbalance other lies in a way that results in the truth in between. The truth is that you can have what you need and what you need is your share and your share is limited by what is needed by others for their share. No collective human government alone can make it possible or impossible for you to have your share of the energy, information and material necessary for optimum existence. You are the one that makes your existence optimal or not by the understanding and control you have of yourself in relation to me, Omega primarily, and to any alpha aspect of me secondarily. The vision that you must seek to understand and to demonstrate is one that makes a good fit of ability and need, supply and demand, environment and organism, the Universe and the individual. Call that vision of holistic fitness the Paragon; its basic ingredients are three structures: iota, alpha, and Omega; and its four functions: "Yea, yea; Nay, nay."

Commentary: In the lesson above, my Omega is telling me that I can have what I need when I need it because there is an order to the good life that is optimum, and it applies to me and to others according to what fits for us at any particular time in our experience. If I make what I want something other than what I need, I set the stage of my experience for extreme errors of too much and too little. Learning how to balance well the errors I experience in a way that results in the truth in between is an ongoing project that depends on my use of the Yoes code. Using my code proactively, I can prime myself for not over or under using reason or appetite, logic or intuition, and service to others or self-serving.

During the early years when I was walking on crutches, I was finding it hard to get to my college classes on time. This was frustrating until I learned how to relax by covertly repeating affirmations that made me feel content regardless of how my environment was challenging me. In those college years of the 1950s, I used comforting statements from the Bible to keep me fearless of being at a disadvantage. I was being prepared to discover the YyNn code for holistic fitness, a default mind-set conducive to feeling at home in the world and to being of service to others. I can only be fit holistically to the extent that I, iota, remember Omega foremost as All and any alpha aspect as a reflection of that Omega totality.

Lesson Five from My Universe to Me about Conflict Resolution

The unresolved conflicts you experience and witness others experiencing are self-created. Faulty mental focus is the basic culprit. Mental focusing is always a matter of some degree of opening and closing, affirming and negating. The conflicts you experience result from mismatching your Yea 1 receptivity to my Nay 1 potency. To harmonize with me as your Universe, you must train yourself to request help from me and then listen to me respectfully and gratefully before making decisions of significant consequence. This attitude helps to align you properly with the each and All of your experience.

Your conscious ego has the perpetual task of harmonizing the each and All of your experience. This tri-unity of your mind as it focuses on both All and some targeted aspect of All, is a model of yourself that you can use to identify and to optimize yourself in relation to the part and Whole of your Self. These three existential spheres interact joyfully as long as you, the one in the middle, make ends meet and unmeet optimally. How well you focus your attention on each and All is what determines the quality of your experience. It is never too late to stop being a victim of your own faulty mental focusing.

There is no conflict in the extra-psychic world that can endure the resolution of intra-psychic conflict. It is only by resolving the conflicts within that you can hope to solve outside problems in a lasting way. Meditate continuously on a template of yourself as a tripartite monad whose median member, iota, is consciously and consistently making the choices that harmonize the flow of information between the alpha and Omega, each and All extremes of your experience.

Commentary: After I graduated from college, I noticed when I was teaching biology to teenagers conflict was the norm. However, I also watched how conflicts tended to be resolved if I, the one in the middle, relaxed and waited until it fit for me to make a move. Students who were either over assertive or over passive were used to moderate each other as I experienced them. I would ask my Universe, Omega, to help me promote a harmonious resolution to whatever conflict was being made manifest. After proactively priming myself with right asking, I would read the feedback from within and from without, and I would know what to say and when to say it. Asking, listening, and timing became my major experimental interests.

The YyNn inner work code is designed to facilitate conflict resolution of all kinds.

Lesson Six from My Universe to Me about Sameness and Difference

There are three fundamental kinds of reality for you to equilibrate optimally moment by moment. The primal reality can be called solar reality. Next, the antithesis of solar reality is lunar reality. The third kind of reality is terrestrial. Terrestrial reality is a synthesis of solar and lunar realities. As your Universe, I am the celestial binary whose solar and lunar sides sandwich you, the earth-like one in between. Your perennial problem is to make your reality, the reality you experience, the best possible synthesis of my realities.

It is easy to err in your reality making because of the ever-present temptation to make too much of one side of me and not enough of the other side of me. The reality you must make if you are to be truly happy and healthy is a periodic motion of waxing and waning that is like the moon in being variable enough yet like the sun in being stable enough. As my image and likeness, you must learn how to be optimally variable/stable. You can learn to avoid chaos and boredom, pain and numbness, by following the example of the earth as it keeps itself optimally poised between the sun and the moon.

To achieve and maintain this critical distance between excess and deficiency, follow the earth like wisdom in between. Your wise use of the YyNn template is the appropriate amount of centrifugal and centripetal force required for the heaven-on-earth state of consciousness.

Commentary: My Universe is my interpretation of the one Universe that you and I share. I call that Universe, Omega. You have your interpretation of the Universe we share, and you have your own name for it. We do not have the same experience of the Universe we share. There are some differences and some similarities. We are unique centers of reference within the same frame of reference we call the Universe.

I use a certain kind of information to help me feel at home in the Universe that I live in. I make an effort every day to consciously prime my subconscious mind to help me find my right place in the Universe, and I am getting feedback every day that helps me to find that right place. When I am there, I attract what is right for me, and I repel what is wrong for me. I know this method works for me, and these lessons are my way of explaining how I am learning from my Universe and you how to be as right as possible with you and my Universe.

I am alpha and Omega intercommunicating in accord with "Yea, yea; Nay, nay."

Lesson Seven from My Universe to Me about Fine-Tuning

Life is like a foot race. Each step must be placed as well as possible. If your steps are placed well enough, you continue to live and flourish. If your steps are placed poorly, you self-destruct. You are born with a tendency to strike and maintain one of three possible paces in the race of life. The three possible paces are minimum, medium, and maximum. You are destined to suffer and die if you follow only one of these paces. The pace you must achieve and maintain to survive in the deadly serious game of life is a pace that is optimum for you at any particular time. An optimum pace can be discovered moment by moment, but it cannot be inherited or preconditioned by others. You must understand your inherited and conditioned tendency to pace your steps falsely and watch to speed them up, to slow them down, or to maintain their speed according to what is optimal for your experiential moment.

I am using the word "step" as a metaphor for choice. You make a choice every moment of your life, and that choice helps to increase, to decrease, or to maintain whichever state you chose before. The state you need is a golden mean between states that are more or less than optimum. What was optimal before may be more or less than optimal now. You must learn to not over or under fixate. The worldview promulgated by modern society is probably false for you. Its values can rarely be dynamic and individual enough to apply truthfully to you. To run well with me, you need to fine tune your steps. Be ready to change in harmony with my changes by programming yourself to be optimally programmed and deprogrammed—encoded as: "Yea, yea; Nay, nay."

Commentary: Early in my adult experience, I learned how to sail. I knew I had found a perfect way for me to be in the world. Sailing was a way I could be close to nature even though I was unable to hike into the natural world of forest and stream where I spent so much of my childhood. Sailing also served as an analogy of how to live by fine-tuning. By fine-tuning my sails in relation to wind and water, I could get where I wanted to go. By fine-tuning my thoughts in relation to my body and the world, I have been able to get what I need.

In 1969, I started a sailing school in San Diego, California, called Harbor Island Sailing Academy, which is still going today under the name of Harbor Sailboats. Two of my favorite activities, sailing and wheelchair tennis, are perfect teachers of the importance of fine-tuning between too much and too little, too soon and too late.

Lesson Eight from My Universe to Me about What Is First

I am the source that you must put first. The world of material appearances that you perceive with your physical senses is a reflection of my invisible order that is perfect. As the source of all that you experience, I am perfect, but your concept of me can be imperfect. You need to be free enough from the objects of material sense to learn how to synchronize your knowing and doing with my knowing and doing. Your psyche must order its steps to dance with the order of my steps. We can sing and dance together as long as you let me lead. Your trouble starts when you, through lack of understanding, lose faith in my lead.

Blind faith is not good enough to change your steps to match mine often enough for continuous health and happiness. So, you must have enough faith to work for understanding by making that the primary use of your attention. If you let me, I will lead you to the information you need for understanding by turning your attention first to me and then to my reflection. The reflection of me that you experience materially will only be as perfect as your alignment with me is during the moment of reflection. It is like considering your relationship to a light behind you before trying to make a shadow on a wall in front of you. Just remember my perfection now, and I will be reflected well enough by you and for you now.

Commentary: In my experience, I am learning how to use the YyNn code to serve as an algorithm for putting first things first. First my attention must go to the Universe with Yea 1, then to a target part of the Universe with yea 2, then to a target with Nay 1, and then back to the Universe with nay 2. This is the meta-technology that helps me to feel well-aligned with the each and All of my experience. Placing my attention on the abstract perfection of the Omega All first, and then targeting some part of all, a person or event that I experience as concrete, helps me to experience that target reflecting what I need to see it reflect.

When I built my tree house in 1976, I was decoding YyNn. I used the information I was receiving from within to guide me in the building of my tree house. To repeat, it had an Omega upper level an alpha lower level and an iota intermediate level which went outside and inside to indicate the binary nature of iota. The boards used in the tree house were old boards salvaged from farms in the neighborhood and new boards from lumber yards.

I am both alpha and Omega, inside and outside, new and used—sometimes more one than the other, sometimes both equally, but, in truth, never too much or too little of either and always enough of both.

Lesson Nine from My Universe to Me about Nature and Culture

Your mission is not to just resolve the conflict between nature and culture; it is to optimize the conflict between nature and culture. This means that the dynamic tension between these two sides of yourself should increase and decrease within certain extremes and be maintained in a way that never sacrifices too much of one side to the other. You are constantly tempted to side with either the natural side of yourself at the expense of the cultivated side or vice versa. The theory that an ideal balance between these two is possible is appealing to you, and you even manage to practice this theory to some extent every day in order to survive.

Your life cycle moves in general from nature to culture and then back to nature again. Even daily you move from the natural state of sleep to the cultivated state of consciousness and then back to sleep again. As you gain a better understanding of these two opposing sides of yourself, you can refine this cyclical process of developing from, and returning to, nature in such a way that you will avoid unnecessary suffering and untimely death. The key to training yourself for optimum balance is the wise use of attention to what is natural and to what is cultural such that each is given a proper voice in the modifying of the other.

Commentary: As a student of biology at the Principia College in the 1950s, I was introduced to ecology. I knew I was at home the minute I was awakened to the concept of "the web of life." I loved the concepts of the ecosphere and the biosphere. I especially liked the way the wet biosphere was poised between the lithosphere and the atmosphere. That was when I first started down the road to a concept of myself as an organic cosmos with a vital middle factor called subjective experience or self-awareness.

I could feel myself expanding. It was, and still is very exhilarating to awaken to a sense of self that is critically related to everything everywhere. I found myself to be a balancing act of expansion and contraction, integration and disintegration, anabolism and catabolism, growth and decay, regeneration and degeneration, and nature and culture—sometimes more to one side than the other, sometimes equal to both, but in truth, never too much or too little of either and always enough of both.

My code for self-making, YyNn is an all-purpose mantra that is the backbone of my conscious life. It optimally connects and disconnects me with all that is from nature and culture, enough of each to not be too much or too little of either. In learning how to think more dialectically, I am becoming less distorted by thinking dualistically. The YyNn code is designed to synthesize the opposites optimally.

Lesson Ten from My Universe to Me about Adaptation

Life is a dynamic process within certain extremes. Words are too static to capture the dynamic truth about life. Words are static symbols. Life is movement and rest. Love me, Omega, your universe, and your love will awaken you to the vital, fresh, dynamic nature of the life process. You and I are the life process when you love me first and foremost. I am the absolute to which you must make relative adjustments. You can choose to harmonize with me and live well or to not harmonize with me and suffer. I want you to want to harmonize with all of me, not just a part of me.

I require that you desire to adapt to the whole Universe, because you are designed for just that kind of adaptation. You will never know how perfectly you can harmonize with each and All until you learn to use YyNn to prove that you are a magnificently designed mechanism for survival. Trusting your inner work, you examine and experiment; you use the field of your experience to test and refine your awareness and behavior, separating the dross from the gold and proving what a glorious creation you are. Only you can verify yourself as the Universe well-individualized and the individual well-universalized.

Commentary: I am a mother-earth-loving pagan and a sky-father-loving Christian. Sometimes I am more one than the other; sometimes I am both equally. But in truth, I am never too much or too little of either and always I am enough of both.

Adaptation is a condition an organism achieves by fitting into its environment well enough to perpetuate itself. It is a quality of fitness similar to the way a shoe fits a foot—well enough to not be too tight or too loose for comfortable and necessary walking.

I am testing a self-programming code for optimal adaptation, a survival code from Matthew 5:37: "Yea, yea; Nay, nay." These are the four basic functions of the Self. I found the structures of the Self in Revelation 1:8: "I am Alpha and Omega." I interpret that to mean the structure of the Self is a tripartite monad whose middle member, iota, is a combination of alpha and Omega. My Self system is based on these statements from the King James Version of the Bible. I repeat both *I am alpha and Omega* and *YyNn* in some form or another throughout this book as a way to reinforce their meanings in my mind and to possibly make them meaningful to you. I am alpha and Omega and YyNn is what I do, and why I do it.

Lesson Eleven from My Universe to Me about Natural Balance

The language of nature is always being spoken to you. You must learn to translate nature's patterns into meanings useful to your stability and survival. The unity in nature indicates the need you have for order. The diversity in nature indicates the need you have for freedom. Yet, it is the balance of natural unity and diversity—the dynamic equilibrium—that is most vital to you. Contemplate the dynamic way a waterfall unites above and below, the way your body's skin moderates influences from the inside and from the outside, the way a rainbow results from an optimum alignment of radiation and moisture via you as an observer, and the multifarious other ways that differences and similarities are created, destroyed, and maintained.

All of your learning efforts should be directed toward understanding and demonstrating how the balance of nature is a sign of your moment-by-moment need for an all-encompassing homeostasis. You must learn how to consciously prime your unconscious with YyNn, the code for the true reflection of Truth. You, iota, are the potential earthlike state of balance between the moonlike, alpha, and the sun-like, Omega, needed for life and consciousness. Following the example of the earth, you become a master at blinking, pulsating, and yo-yoing, that is, a master at optimally balancing Omega's sameness and alpha's differences in your here-and-now experience.

Commentary: The balance of nature, as applied to my experience, is a principle I use for spiritual exercise. My health of mind, spirit, and body is a type of homeostasis. It is a steady state of rest and motion, sameness and difference, unity and variety at both the macro and micro levels of my existence. I am body and world, the individual and the Universe harmonized by my spiritual practice with YyNn.

This kind of YyNn thinking has helped me to never miss a day of work in more than fifty years. I taught biology for a decade, taught sailing for another decade, ran my own stress management consultancy for ten years, and ran a wheelchair tennis program for fifteen years without missing one session. YyNn is the essence of my work ethic.

Natural balance, as it is displayed by living organisms in relation to their environment, is a paradoxical condition of remaining the same by not changing too much or too little. My heaven-on-earth mind-set, based on my decoding of YyNn, is analogous to the balance of nature. As the balance of nature makes life possible, balancing the opposites makes my life meaningful and purposeful. I am learning how to exemplify the YyNn code for heaven on earth.

Lesson Twelve from My Universe to Me about Positive and Negative

As you become more conscious, you realize the responsibility you have to develop cognitive strategies that will help you to improve the quality of your conscious experience. You will probably start with choosing to be more positive about the way you think. You will notice how negative thinking results in anxious feelings and positive thinking results in confident, relaxed feelings.

Eventually you will see that in the realm of thinking and feeling, as in the realm of numbers, positive is no better than negative—both are necessary. However, in the realm of thinking and feeling, for most people the negative occurs more involuntarily than the positive, and the positive must be consciously chosen to compensate for, and to counterbalance, the negative. Once you understand this, you have the problem of figuring out how much and what kind of positive thinking and feeling is needed to counterbalance the particular negativity you are experiencing at any particular time.

Religion is one of the ancient psychological solutions to this problem. In most religions, thought and feeling are directed away from the predominately negative conditions of material experience toward a positive, spiritual ideal. Ultimately, you realize that negative conditions are here to stay, but they can be moderated so well that the end result is really something better than the unrealistic ideals of organized religions and moral philosophies. Of course, then comes the sobering realization that there will be no final victory, no rest from the constant demand to balance positive and negative optimally. Only your own reason and intuition tested in the fire of challenging experiences can help you solve the dilemma of finding out how much yes and no fit for your here-and-now experience.

Commentary: I think I started to graduate from false dualism to the dialectic in 1955, when I was twenty years old. I was just starting with a dualistic system of thought and wondering why I could not accept the way spirituality was postulated—not just as antagonistic to sensuality, but to be right and sensuality to be wrong. The spiritual discipline required by this system was useful to me for several years, but I knew I was destined to move toward something more holistic and ecological with a well-balanced concept of spirituality and sensuality.

After searching extensively, I asked God, my Universe, for help. My subsequent inspiration guided me to Matthew 5:37: "Let your communication be Yea, yea; Nay, nay." I was on my way to the heaven-on-earth dialectic with iota as the synthesis of alpha and Omega, the self-theory and inner-work practice I needed.

Lesson Thirteen from My Universe to Me about Right Info Flow

Your attention is a gateway, a threshold that moderates the flow between the inner and the outer sides of yourself. Your consciousness is a semipermeable membrane that is conditioned more or less optimally for the inflow of what you need in and the outflow of what you need out. You have the potential for securing the necessary inflow and outflow. All of the stuff you experience is either needed in, out, or in between at any particular moment. You must learn to distinguish between what is needed inside, outside, and in between. Of course, this is impossible from a rational standpoint because of the infinitely varied forms of stuff you experience and because of your inherited tendencies and past conditioning, which tempt you to believe falsely about what is needed inside, outside, and in between.

Reason is limited and your intuition needs to be reactivated in accord with the experiential goal of optimum info flow: upward and downward, backward and forward, in and out, and side to side. Both sound reasoning and truth-inspired insights are constantly needed to help you experience the flow of information, energy, and materials from where it is not needed to where it is needed.

What you need to ingest and egest materially and mentally is always, in some degree, a matter of the moment and never something that can be completely predetermined or fixed. Reactivate your instinct for homing in on exactly what you need when you need it. How do you do that? You meditate on "Yea, yea; Nay, nay," the code for the golden mean. It is a dynamic state of optimum exchange between the alpha and Omega extremes of your experience as iota. The wisdom of dialectical optimism must become programmed into your subconscious mind by your conscious mind to the exclusion of, and deprogramming of, diabolical dualism.

Commentary: I like to think of my experience as a state of information flow into and out of my mind, from and to other minds with the sole purpose of making the best possible experience the most probable experience for myself and others. The information code YyNn is designed for this purpose and so far it is proving to be right for me.

I believe the YyNn code I am testing is possibly the right default mind-set for the future of life on earth. The mental discipline required for proving it depends on a special calling, a readiness within that is predetermined. Of this, I am certain.

Lesson Fourteen from My Universe to Me about Yes and No

I am teaching you how to be a well-integrated and eternal cosmos instead of a fragmented, mortal chaos. The one-to-one, inner relationship between you, iota, and me, Omega, must be the basic way you organize your sense of reality. Any lesser relationship must be secondary and minor in comparison. Resist the temptation to be overspecialized. Consciously visualize the perfect integration of each and All; see each as All uniquely reflected. You experience me in a light that is colored by your previous interpretations. You have created the quality of your experience by the quality of your moment-by-moment interpretations.

The only opportunity you have to improve your experience is now. Each conscious moment is a chance to reach the iota point, your right place, by equilibrating alpha and Omega optimally. Watch your conscious threshold; condition it to yea and nay, affirm and negate, optimally. Homeostasis and equanimity are impossible for you to find and maintain without first learning how to coordinate your yes and no thoughts in a way that fits the moment. By saying "Yes" to me first, you set the stage of your conscious experience for having "yes" said to you by an appropriate other. The way you consciously remember me, your sense of All, determines how well each aspect of me treats you. If you remember to love me, Omega, foremost, you will be loved enough by appropriate alphas.

Love All well, and you will be loved well by others. Love and resist, attract and repel, as you would be loved and resisted, attracted and repelled by others. Meditate on "Yea, yea; Nay, nay," the code for loving and resisting, attracting and repelling, in golden proportions.

Commentary: I am Yoes, a synthesis of yes and no. How well I synthesize yes and no depends on how well I apply YyNn, the code for optimal yes and no sorting of impressions from within and from without. As a result of applying YyNn to my experience, I attract what I need and repel what I do not need.

Just as the evolution of species results from the environment selecting for and against types of organisms, so my own evolution depends on selecting for what is good for me and against what is not good for me. My yes and no determines who I am and what I can do. What is true for me is true for you also in a way unique to you. I am self-referential because I know only from my own perspective and from my own assimilation of information. Reducing everything to information shared by alpha mind and Omega mind helps me, iota mind—an alpha/Omega interface—to keep a heaven-on-earth mind-set of right yes and no info sorting.

Lesson Fifteen from My Universe to Me about the Ultimate Balancing Act

You and I are valuable to each other. As the Omega level of you that is greater, I give you just what you need so you can give lesser ones just what they need. If you feel insecure, it is because you are putting too much trust in the reflections of the lesser principle and not enough trust in the ideals of the greater principle. Any person, book, human institution, drug, diet, or exercise, can help you only to the extent that you are right with me, Omega, the greater principle. By expecting too much of the lesser principle, whose evidence you can see materially, and not trusting enough in me, Omega, the greater principle, whose evidence you cannot see materially, you create all kinds of unnecessary limitations for yourself.

Your genuine inner development is a result of becoming less and less dependent upon particular finite relationships and more and more dependent upon your sense of what is true about your relationship to me—the Infinite and Eternal One. Your primary need as iota, a self-balancing state of consciousness, is to get your experience of the lesser principle, alpha, to harmonize with your concept of the greater principle, Omega. Prepare yourself for this ultimate balancing act by proactively imagining each and All, alpha and Omega uniquely and perfectly coinciding in your moment-by-moment experience as iota, the intermediate interface interpolated optimally between alpha and Omega.

Commentary: Some sailboats are self-righting—they cannot tip too far to one side and capsize. The weight in the boat's keel counterbalances the force of the wind in the sails enough to spill the wind from the sails before the boat reaches the critical point where capsizing is inevitable. Living organisms also have a kind of self-righting capacity.

To be alive, organisms, including humans, have to operate within a critical zone of not too much and not too little heat, moisture, nutrients, waste products, energy, and information. The ultimate balancing act is by the mind that discovers it is poised between the each and All of its experience. The YyNn code is essential for this ultimate balancing act. It is an efficiency booster code I use for the conscious programming of my subconscious mind, helping me to achieve and maintain the balance I need to survive and thrive.

My ongoing intention is to make enough of the alpha aspects I focus upon and to make enough of the Omega source of the alpha aspects to not make too much or too little of either, and always enough of both, relative to my here-and-now experience as iota, the ultimate balancing fulcrum of authentic existence.

Lesson Sixteen from My Universe to Me about Expanding and Contracting

Your personal consciousness is individual, but it is continuous with all that is universal and particular. Your self-awareness is dependent upon my light, yet it is conceived in darkness. It develops by expanding, yet it must contract as much and as often as it expands. The perennial purpose of your iota consciousness must be to expand and contract in optimum synchronization with Omega, the greater conscious sphere containing it, and with alpha, the less conscious sphere it contains. As your Universe, my conscious sphere of invisible, invariable, and Self-created light (whose symbol is the sun in the sky) contains your personal consciousness, and your personal consciousness contains a less conscious sphere of more or less visible, reflected light whose symbol is the moon.

The earth, partaking of both the sun's creativity and the moon's receptivity, symbolizes your personal, subjective consciousness as distinct from Omega and alpha—that which is more self-aware and that which is less self-aware. The earth's rotations and revolutions in relation to the sun and the moon, creating days, months and years, are visible manifestations of the pulsating and rhythmical ways your personal consciousness receives and creates by expanding and contracting, affirming and negating, attracting and repelling. It is important to understand that your consciousness, the means whereby you experience anything, is not explainable in purely rational, literal terms. To figure out what your personal consciousness is and how to optimize it, you need the kind of insights and metaphors only revealed to sincere, open-minded seekers of the kind of truth that results from using excess and deficiency to moderate each other optimally.

Commentary: I interpret what my Universe is saying to me as a type of pattern recognition. The pattern of expansion and contraction first got my attention when I started lifting weights as a teenager to improve my appearance. My muscles, extensors and flexors, responded well to the weight resistance. Using reps and sets of exercises, I learned firsthand about conditioning. Later when I started my inner development, I used the pattern of sets of reps in my meditation exercises.

For me, this has been very important, because it means I can synchronize my inner fitness work with my outer fitness work to get the best possible holistic fitness result. Today on my hand bike, I climbed a steep, mile-long hill, synchronizing my YyNn mantra with my breathing in and out and with my pulling and pushing arm movements. I also do this when I eat, swim, lift weights, and play tennis. Yea Omega for the YyNn mantra I can use anytime and anyplace to help set my mind for being a person who is well-balanced and complete!

Lesson Seventeen from My Universe to Me about Yielding and Standing Firm

Watchfulness is the price you pay for consciousness. In your more unconscious state, you were protected more by instinct and social regulations. Now that you are becoming too conscious to blindly obey or rebelliously disobey the rules needed to regulate less conscious people, you must discover rules that fit you as an individual in relation to me, your Universe. You will meet resistance that will tempt you to fight when you need to forgive and submit, and you will meet adulation that will tempt you to acquiesce when you should stand firm.

To maintain quality control over your conscious experience, you need to train yourself to become optimally yielding and firm as encoded in the YyNn algorithm I have given you for optimal self-programming and self-deprogramming. Only by meditating properly can consciousness modify itself in such a way that it achieves and maintains an optimum increase and decrease of itself.

You must be willing to lose your control in order to regain it. By meditating on the Paragon model of the Self as iota, coexisting harmoniously with alpha and Omega, you consciously prime yourself for making the best possible decision moment by moment. The practice of subordinating your ego to your sense of me, Omega, as All, by asking me for guidance, and by thanking and praising me, helps you develop receptivity that hears both the voice of reason and the voice of instinct. Your value to yourself and to others is in direct proportion to how well you equilibrate appetite and reason, desire and conscience, selfishness and selflessness, alpha and Omega.

Commentary: Learning how and when to submit has been one of my hardest lessons to learn. I am just beginning to master the submissive state of mind, because it is in my genes and my upbringing to fight for my rights and for my place in the sun. However, as I am slowly learning how to balance all the opposites, I am learning how to fight or to back down according to what fits each new situation.

I am a fighter and a lover, sometimes more one than the other, sometimes both equally; but in truth, I am neither too much nor too little like either and always enough like both.Iota, my human ego, the interface factor in my experience, must learn how to yield to Omega and to stand firm for alpha, a servant to All, in order to be a master when needed by any part of All.

Lesson Eighteen from My Universe to Me about Lovemaking

You, iota, must learn how to mate with me, Omega, by matching your Yea 1 to my Nay 1 and your nay 2 to my yea 2; only then can you properly match your Nay 1 to alpha's Yea 1 and your yea 2 to alpha's nay 2. This is the golden meaning of "Let your communication be Yea, yea; Nay, nay: for whatsoever is more than these cometh of evil [error]."

Let your hands represent a handbook of life making. As your left hand is opening (Yea 1), your right hand is entering (Nay 1); as your left hand is closing (nay 2), your right hand is exiting (yea 2). This process of your right hand entering and exiting your left hand as it opens and closes is symbolic for the life-making process. In truth, this is how I, Omega, relate to you, iota, and how you, iota, relate to alpha. The full YyNn sequence is always from iota in relation to Omega (Yea 1), iota in relation to alpha (yea 2), iota in relation to alpha (Nay 1), and iota in relation to Omega (nay 2).

You can use these symbols as you meditate on the Paragon model of the Self that has Omega making love to iota and iota making love to alpha. In YyNn code, life is a result of a three-way lovemaking process with alpha and Omega on each end and iota in the middle. Omega is the masculine principle, alpha is the feminine principle, and iota is the androgynous principle. In the handbook of life making, the palm and each finger symbolize basic life principles. The palm is Omega, the fingers are types of alphas, and the thumb is iota. The type of metaphysical exercises called *rainbows* in YyNn code are done by matching thumb to fingers in a way that symbolizes making the too little more enough, the enough to remain enough, and the too much less enough. Eventually I will introduce you to more of the handbook and the way to do metaphysical exercises in sync with physical exercises for the purpose of holistic fitness.

Commentary: My life has been an ongoing attempt to reconcile spirituality and sexuality. Religion and sex have been my main interests and influences since I was first introduced to them. I tried to go all the way to religion and away from sex, but that was too boring and abstract. Then I went too far into sex and that got me into trouble with a puritanical establishment. Now I have a good way to balance sex and religion by using them to modify each other optimally as a vision I call the Paragon.

When I am praying, I am remembering how life is made by lovemaking. My prayers are a form of lovemaking and my lovemaking is a form of praying. My code is a form of tantric yoga, using the energy of sex for achieving inner self-development. YyNn is my code for making life better by visualizing Omega making love to iota as iota makes love to alpha, a loving household-of-three vision of the Self. Jesus said, "The kingdom of heaven is like unto leaven hid in three measures of meal, till the whole was leavened" (Matthew 13:33).

Lesson Nineteen from My Universe to Me about Sophrosyne

You are a cosmic agent free to choose at any moment who you will serve. Serve the Whole, or the part—more or less than is optimum and you will suffer. How can you know whether to expand your attention to the whole that I am or to contract your attention to some part of me? Is it time to focus your attention on some alpha center of reference or to the Omega frame of reference? What is an optimum state of consciousness? How much does optimum consciousness depend upon freedom of attention? What practices keep your attention free for the control that truly fits the moment you are experiencing? Is logic enough? Is instinct or intuition available to aid logic?

The ancient Greeks used the word *sophrosyne* to stand for an optimum equilibration of life's variables. Socrates, in Plato's dialogue, *Charmides* concludes, "I have failed utterly to discover what *sophrosyne* is." Socrates knew how to use logic to prove that words can never discover the exact truth about anything. He used words to reveal the limits of logic and to thereby clear the way for fitting insights to unfold spontaneously. Actually, it is only necessary to meditate more and more on "Yea, yea; Nay, nay," the code for *sophrosyne*, to experience more of it. Attending to the YyNn vision helps you to have enough of the kind of experience that feels and looks like an optimum balance of life's variables.

Commentary: As a teacher of biology, sailing, tennis, and meditation, I have experimented with temperance, another word for *sophrosyne*. My genetic and social conditioning helped me to be a fighter, but eventually I had to learn how to control my temper. I found that teaching required me to remain cool when tempted to get impatient but forceful enough to not put my students to sleep. It was a balancing act, as all of my life experiences have been and continue to be. Finding the way to accept or assert, temper down or temper up, in accord with what fits the moment is the purpose of my meditation system.

I love Plato for introducing me to *sophrosyne*, a name for something that I believe to be the most important lesson my Universe is teaching me. I am learning that life and consciousness are a result of a certain kind of balance of something from above and something from below. I am the result of that special kind of balance, and so are you. I like to call it heaven on earth. The only problem is that we have only enough of it to get started on our own as individuals. To refine what has been given to each of us is, I believe, our ultimate task—the task of making gold out of physical stuff from below and metaphysical stuff from above.

Lesson Twenty from My Universe to Me about Right Request

Fitness is a good word for the condition you must gain and maintain. Only with my help, as your Universe, can you demonstrate the intellectual, emotional, and physical fitness that is true for you as an individual. Fitness is a matter of your individual needs and abilities in relation to the needs and abilities of others. Without the inspiration you receive by putting the true model of us, the Paragon, foremost in your thoughts, it is rare for you to optimally fit your abilities and needs to the needs and abilities of others.

There is a standard of fitness that applies to you in relation to all others. You can learn about this true standard by studying patterns of nature and culture. The human standards that conditioned you as a child and the human standards that prevail in your present environment are likely to mislead you and to fail as fit guides for your present overall fitness needs. Defer to the model of the Universe and the individual, Omega, and alpha reciprocating optimally through you, iota, at the point of Golden Section. Meditate on this Self model enough and it will be the operating standard of fitness in your life, supplanting any false standard of fitness.

Ask me, Omega, to help you to make the too much less enough and the too little more enough and the fit to remain fit by increasing and decreasing enough. If this concept of enough is too vague for you, relax. It is not too vague for me. Let me help you to make the too vague exact enough and the too exact vague enough. The right request is your responsibility. My responsibility is to respond well to your request.

Commentary: I have experimented extensively with asking Omega, my name for God, for guidance, and the results have been very convincing. The results have not necessarily convinced me that God hears my request, but they have convinced me that I relax and make better decisions because of my requests for help from Omega.

One example of how this way of relaxing saved my life is what took place on a freeway covered with ice and snow. I thought I was past the part of the highway that was slick, but I wasn't. My car started to spin in circles and went into the muddy divider. I said, "Help, dear God." My car continued to spin over to the other side of the freeway, heading in the opposite direction yet fitting safely between other moving cars. If I had frozen up and tried to control the car, it probably would have turned over. Being able to relax under pressure is a result of using cognitive strategies well. YyNn is my all-purpose cognitive strategy.

Lesson Twenty-One from My Universe to Me about Oscillation

In the Yoes meditation system, I am the Whole called Omega and any part of me is called alpha. The synthesis of alpha and Omega is called iota. Iota emerges from a certain kind of alpha to become more like Omega and then submerges to become more like alpha. This oscillation process is the way iota is transformed from being lopsided, bottom-heavy, and top-heavy to being well-balanced and complete. The practice needed by you to reach this optimum state of increase and decrease is based on the encoded YyNn mantra, as decoded by you, an iota I have selected for that purpose.

The enlightenment that came to you when you were meditating on the YyNn mantra in the desert was a break-through experience triggered by synchronizing the yeas and nays of the encoded mantra with your inhalations and exhalations, such that the first "Yea" meant taking in, the second "yea" meant taking out, the first "Nay" meant putting in, and the second "nay" meant putting out.

This order was later discovered by you as the order of the human heart's left atrium: taking in fresh blood = Yea 1; the right atrium taking out stale blood = yea 2; the left ventricle putting in fresh blood = Nay 1; the right ventricle putting out stale blood = nay 2. The heartbeat pattern and the way your lungs circulate fresh air in and stale air out are symbols for the basic four functions of the Self and a foundation for practicing Yoes meditation.

Commentary: I am a harmonic oscillator operating on the basis of the YyNn algorithm. Using this inner-work procedure has helped me to find my place in the world. By transforming how I see the world and my place in it, I have a more friendly world/self-experience. It is not easy to do this while living in a wheelchair, but I have been blessed by a persistent spirit. I have developed the YyNn mind-set to the point where it is now making the world conform to meeting my needs in fascinating, and adventurous ways. More and more I am discovering that I can make my world the best of all possible worlds.

As my inner communication with the various sides and levels of my inner self continues to improve, I, iota, am confident that the best possible communication between my higher Omega Mind and my lower alpha mind can be established. I am learning how to use YyNn communication to bring about the best kind of oscillation of information between the alpha part and the Omega Whole of my experience. YyNn is a vision of my intention to make the best possible communication between myself and others the most probable communication.

Lesson Twenty-Two from My Universe to Me about the Opposites

You are losing your confidence in material appearances. You are gaining confidence in your own creative power to be the master of material appearances instead of their servant. A metaphysical ideal is forming within you that will give birth to improved physical conditions. You are beginning to tap reservoirs of heretofore unknown wisdom and power. You are learning how to place wise limits on your appetites and creative expressions. Your understanding of truth-making is developing in time to avoid the errors of false pride and ignorance.

Your soul is safe as long as you remember to oscillate between the opposites of your experience. Soul is a good word for your developing psyche. It is distinct from what is eternally true as an ideal and what is apparent as real. Your job is to master the process of equilibrating the ideal and the real by not making too much or too little of either. Your soul has the eternal task of using the real to figure out what is ideal and using the ideal to improve the real. To do this you must work to replace dualistic values with dialectical and ecological values.

An example of false, dualistic values is the belief that good and evil are opposites like light and darkness. Ecologically, light and darkness are understood to be of equal value, with an optimum increase of one and decrease of the other being necessary for life on earth. Using material appearances to access the truth behind all such appearances is the way to make the material order conform more closely to the ecological truth. A dynamic, ecological vision of right timing and placing is yours to internalize. As a rainbow maker, you can learn to match thing and place, organism and environment, in a way that is ecologically optimum.

Commentary: When I started to consciously develop my own system of inner self-work, I had been mainly influenced by Mary Baker Eddy and her religion, Christian Science. Her concept of "mortal mind" was my main point of difference with her. I replaced "mortal mind" with alpha mind, the human mind with iota mind, and the divine Mind with Omega Mind. That way I had a spectrum, a coherent system of twenty-four levels in three octaves that could be harmonized by iota, the mind in the middle.

Later, I found other systems of esoteric thought that had concepts of the levels of consciousness, but none of them appealed to me as much as my own system. I worked out the basics of my system by 1975 as a result of my desert epiphany while meditating with "Yea, yea; Nay, nay," my all-purpose mantra and self-identifying and self-optimizing code. "I am alpha and Omega" means to me that I am composed of opposites that I can learn to harmonize using the YyNn code.

Lesson Twenty-Three from My Universe to Me about the Rainbow

Our relationship is like a rainbow when you position yourself optimally between the light and dark principles. If your position is not optimum, you experience too much of one extreme and not enough of the other extreme. As you learn to understand the law of natural balance and how to apply it in your experience, you will make rainbowlike relationships continually out of what would otherwise be relationships that favor one side of your experience too much and the other side of your experience too little. Without understanding, you are vulnerable to superstitions and prejudices. Superstitions and prejudices are false beliefs you can have about yourself and others.

It is easy, due to the paradoxical way things appear to you, to believe that you are either more or less responsible than you really are for either the heaven or hell you experience. Just as when you experience nature's rainbow it is because of where you are as an observer in relation to sunlight and moisture, so it is with all of your relationships. The basic ingredients are not your responsibility, but how the ingredients are related in your experience is your responsibility. Every choice you make is either more or less adaptive to you being related to the each and All of your experience in a way that is as beautiful and harmonious as the rainbow.

Commentary: Iota is to alpha and Omega as a rainbow observer is to a rain cloud and sunlight. I ask Omega, my Universe, to help me understand myself and my purpose in life. I then get inspiration from patterns in nature such as the rainbow-making pattern of three main ingredients, each of which has to be at the angle necessary for making rainbow beauty. All of my inner work is based on this idea of right arrangement of me in relation to an alpha target of reference and the Omega frame of reference. I visualize an optimum flow of information from Omega to me and from me to alpha and back again.

I use this vision when I am playing wheelchair tennis. It helps me to relax and to enjoy the oscillating process of the tennis ball moving back and forth. It helps me to think less about winning and losing and more about making the best possible dynamic between my opponent and the Universe with me as the mediating fulcrum in between. The rally becomes more important than the score.

I believe that the rainbow exists as a symbol for us to use in our efforts to become well-balanced and complete. The ingredients for heaven on earth are given. How well those ingredients are arranged is up to each of us.

Lesson Twenty-Four from My Universe to Me about Wisdom

The model of the Self that I am teaching you, and its YyNn method, are impossible to describe in a completely literal way. Your mind must take the words I speak to you and use them as pieces of a puzzle that you can solve. I can help you more and more efficiently as you get more and more of the puzzle pieces into their proper places. As your understanding improves, you will be aware of how to interpret anything I say in a way that will facilitate your comprehension of how you ought to be related to the each and All of your experience at any particular time.

Your true development is in the direction of being able to turn everything you experience into something of value. In all of your experiences, it is your own interpretation of them that determines their value to you. Your experiences are only wasted to the extent that you do not interpret them wisely. I provide the wisdom, which your experience alone can uncover for you if it is consciously used for that purpose. Wisdom is what you use to distinguish between what is true for you and what is false for you. Wisdom is immediate, creative, and practical; it is temperate because it is a way between erroneous extremes, and dynamic because it is adaptive to changes inside and outside. Seek the way my wisdom points out for you here and now, and you will find yourself centered between too soon and too late, too little and too much.

Commentary: Wisdom is what it takes to make the best possible life the most probable life. By what standard is a life the best possible? To live long enough to reproduce is the standard used by biological evolution. The standard I use to measure my success is how well I fill the niche I believe is predetermined for me. To find and fill that niche, I do attention control exercises with YyNn.

How well do I serve the needs of myself and others? In my sailing school, I put service before profit. That worked well until I incorporated and gave up my control of the budget. The board wanted to cut back on the quality of sailboats we bought so they could make more money. I sold my shares to another board member, because I could not accept the concept of profit before quality of service. One of the board members eventually bought out all of the other board members, and he put quality of service back as a priority. The sailing school is still going as Harbor Sailboats in San Diego, California, claiming me as the founder and the date I started the school, 1969, as the founding date.

The wise use of YyNn helps to improve the quality of my service to others.

Lesson Twenty-Five from My Universe to Me about Receptivity

I am always nourishing you according to your needs as an individual. Each moment I send you what will promote your genuine development. You are learning to wait on me. Putting aside your preconceived notions of right and wrong, true and false, desirable and undesirable, you are in a pure state of receptivity. I come to you with what fits for now. Condition yourself to expect the best from me, your Universe, but never think you know exactly what that best is before it is needed. Learning to live inspiration by inspiration is dependent on your proactive and covert rehearsals of the YyNn code for heaven on earth.

I have just the resources you need. You will never know how well I provide for you until you learn how to pay attention to me. Wait patiently to be received well by others, but never hesitate to receive me well. Our each-All Self system, as you experience it, is regulated primarily by your receptivity. Receiving me well frees you from the fear of not being received well by others. It is easy to open yourself to others when they are open to you. The true test of character is how to remain open to the whole Universe while you are being ignored or hated by someone from whom you want love and respect. Your mission is to love All primarily, and then you will see how to be of help to the particular individual who will draw out your best and love you for it.

Commentary: It took me a while to learn how important it is to put learning before doing, listening before speaking, and receiving before sending. The YyNn code is based on putting openness to the Universe first; just remembering to do that is a key factor in making my life work the way I believe it is supposed to.

Finding a job that I like and a place to live that I like has always been easy for me, and I think that is because I expect the Universe, my God, Omega, to have the best possible place for me at any particular moment of my experience. I proactively program for that possibility, and I get feedback confirming that I am on the right track. YyNn is a GPS for my inner computer.

One example of this is the place I lived on Coast Walk in La Jolla, California. From 1965 to 1978, I lived a stone's throw from one of the most beautiful sights in the world. I was away from car traffic, looking out my bay window to a stretch of Pacific Ocean and La Jolla Shores that never ceased to inspire me. Other examples are my tree house and my 46-foot sloop, "Cholita," both fabulous examples of romantic places to live and play. Yea, Omega!

Lesson Twenty-Six from My Universe to Me about the Sex Act

Our Omega-Iota-Alpha Self system is a macro-bio-microcosmic Self system, and like the Sun-Earth-Moon system, it is designed to be free from monotony and chaos. We are truly a Cosmos, centered wherever you are consciously loving with a pure heart and reasoning with a clear head. I always give you the kind of light you need to find the appropriate balance of sensitivity and power, tenderness and strength. Scanning for my lead with no presumptions, you become the servant of the truth-making process. Truth-making is how we should fit together in the here and now of your experience. You are designed to love the Truth and to make truth out of any erroneous deviation you experience.

Harmony is the true state of things that you make by equilibrating false extremes truthfully. As your cosmic complement, I expect a proper minus for my plus and a proper plus for my minus. All of your troubles are simply a sign of your inefficiency in matching your Yea to my Nay and your nay to my yea. Our communication can be cosmic copulation, an intercommunication that is meta-sexual intercourse reproducing life through the love of truth. The meditation exercises I am teaching you are recapitulations of the macro-bio-microcosmic sex act that is life. Meditate on your Self as a tripartite system of intercommunicating sex partners that live to make life and consciousness by loving the truth about each other.

Commentary: Mind and information, minus and plus, yes and no, self and other, attraction and repulsion, affirmation and negation, and the feminine principle and the masculine principle are all ways of describing the essentials of the life-making process. YyNn is a code for optimizing that process.

You notice that I do not try to explain why I use two of the Jesus sayings to make my case for a system of inner self-work. There are other Jesus sayings that support what I am presenting, but I do not want to get into that in this book. I am trying to provide a basis for keeping the work of cultivating consciousness as simple and as coherent as possible. Most of the Jesus sayings are useful to the inner-work project I am conducting, but some of them are too dualistic to be consistent with the understanding I am getting from that project.

I believe some of what Jesus is reputed to have said is a result of being misinterpreted by dualistically minded translators who felt a need to take sides with spirit against the flesh rather than figure out a form of disambiguation that makes friends instead of enemies out of spirit and flesh, spirituality and sensuality.

Lesson Twenty-Seven from My Universe to Me about Sharing

I am the Whole you must love foremost before you can be assured of relating well to anything less than the whole of me. Cultivate a sense of each and All being optimally connected and disconnected. Imagine that you are always receiving optimally from the one excessive and sending optimally to the one deficient. Play Robin Hood as a meditation exercise. As you follow your inhalations and exhalations, meditate on taking from the able and giving to the needy. Repeat this vision of optimum sharing over and over just as you breathe in and out, over and over. Your psyche's health is as dependent on a vision of optimum sharing as your soma is dependent on respiration.

Optimum sharing is the golden meaning of your existence. Your existence can only be optimum to the extent that your sharing with the each and All of your experience is optimum. How do you know when your sharing is optimum? You don't! It is enough that you want your sharing to be optimum more than you want anything else.

By meditating often enough on a vision of optimum sharing, e.g. the Paragon, you set the stage of your experience for spontaneous unfoldments of material evidence supporting that vision. What you meditate on most, you tend to materialize most. Have faith in your efforts to renew yourself from within.

Commentary: I saw a video recently of a young ape playing with a dog and sharing its food with the dog. It was an ongoing relationship between these two angelic creatures, playing and sharing food. I felt inspired by this simple yet profound way of relating between two extremely different creatures. The ape was playing a vital role, a bridge between its whole environment and this dog—part of the whole. By sharing its food with the dog, it established a vital connection with the whole of which it and the dog are parts. I cannot think of a better example of how we all should be living.

The iota principle that I am so enthusiastically presenting is my name for the Christ principle. It is an interface designed to be used as a filter for sharing the best from above and below. My spinal cord tumor was a single structure when it was first removed; by the time it was removed again, it was a tripartite structure. It may have been my own way of expressing a truth about myself as a synthesis of heaven and earth, my ego learning how to be a means of sharing Omega with alpha in a way that made enough of both and not too much or too little of either.

Lesson Twenty-Eight from My Universe to Me about Heaven and Hell

It is important that you develop the power of your "yea" and "nay" thoughts. It is the way you can eventually optimize and complete yourself. Use "yea" and "nay" as tools for the inner work you can always do, to improve your inner experience primarily and to subsequently improve your outer experience. By using your "yea" to affirm the reality of the perfect fit and using your "nay" to reject any suggestion to the contrary, you free yourself for your true destiny.

Consciously build your sense of world-mind-body fitness from within, and you will eventually see this ideal appear in the world around you. Once you are master of your inner life, you will never again be a slave to, or victim of, material circumstances. You will be the anointed one saving your inner and outer worlds from the imperfections you have unwittingly imposed upon them.

The only hell you must escape is the one into which you have allowed yourself and your concept of others to fall. Your timely "Yea" will keep you from the hell of deficiency, and your timely "Nay" will keep you from the hell of excess. The appropriate use of affirmation and negation, yes and no, will extract you from the false state of mind called hell and enable you to build your own heaven on earth.

Commentary: I have spent my whole life dealing with serious adversity. As a child, I was subject to emotional abuse by my alcoholic father, whom I loved very much. I could tell it was a demon of some kind, which I did not identify with him as a person. It was some kind of imposition, a false belief acquired as a child, and/or a character weakness that he did not know how to fix. His early demise served as an example to guide me away from unhealthy dependence on alcohol and tobacco, as well as any psychoactive drugs.

The other lifetime adversity I have been dealing with is chronic spinal cord disease resulting in paraplegia. I am being forced to learn how to walk the YyNn talk using YyNn as my spiritual backbone.

"Sweet are the uses of adversity, which like the toad, ugly and venomous, wears yet a jewel in its head." Shakespeare

"Yea, yea; Nay, nay" is my pearl of great price. I have paid a great price for YyNn, but it has been essential to my cultivation of a heaven-on-earth state of conscious experience instead of the hell on earth experience I could have had.

Lesson Twenty-Nine from My Universe to Me about Good and Evil

The diabolical extremes you experience of too much and too little and of too soon and too late are the result of your own ignorance of how to harmonize the way you and I, the individual and the Universe, change moment by moment. Your inner evolution is in overcoming the diabolical belief that one side of existence is always good and the other side is always evil. By thinking of life's extremes as irreconcilable opposites you set the stage of your conscious experience for war. To get yourself harmoniously balanced you must recognize the limits of your perceptions and develop concepts of value that do not fix differences into fixed good and bad molds.

There is a standard of good in relation to human experience, but it is dynamic and ineffable and only discovered consciously and consistently by the individual human being who knows how to cultivate optimum receptivity. The good is always approximated by the individual in some degree, as are the true and the beautiful. But the true good and beautiful are never opposed by an absolute antagonist called the devil or evil except in the imagination of a self-deceived human being. True goodness and beauty are intermediate values that exist only in relation to some individual conscious of being in between opposing extremes. The light principle is only good if you make it so by the way you choose to relate to it. The dark principle is only bad if you make it so by the way you choose to relate to it. The experiential opposites need a relative equilibrator who understands how to make truth out of plus and minus errors, how to make life out of birth and death, and how to make a healthy ego out of righteous indignation and ignorant complacency.

Commentary: I remember when I first started to contemplate the possibility that my culture was wrong about "good and evil." What caused me to change my mind was a result of contemplating how, from a biological perspective, good is an optimum state between lethal extremes. For example, a plant needs light and water, not too much or too little of either, but enough of both. The zone between excess and deficiency is a truth-making zone of optimum sameness and difference.

When I program myself with YyNn, I am programming with an ideal vision of myself as a spectrum or continuum. Iota, the middle octave of the spectrum is a zone of optimum balancing of the alpha and Omega octaves, the opposing ends of the spectrum. I visualize the flow of information needed to make me, iota in the middle, right with the Omega and alpha ends above and below, in back and in front, outside and inside, to the left and to the right.

Lesson Thirty from My Universe to Me about Perfection

You are the way I become a new consciousness of my Self. Because of you, I have a new way to both know and show that which is truly excellent, beautiful, good, and true. I have designed you to be a balancing fulcrum with the awareness of what it means to make the best out of every imperfect deviation. There is no such thing as static perfection.

Perfection is always a matter of the individual making the best out of what is by changing what has been in a way that fits with what will be. Perfection is you mediating optimally between the up-down, forward-backward, inside-outside, and side-to-side opposites of your experience. You are the way my infinitude is given a definite experience.Perfection is a quality within a zone of variations that you can individualize, understand, and demonstrate ad infinitum. You are the perfect equalizer of all that is more and less than what is just right. Cultivate a sense of what it means to be the perfect equalizer. It means sameness and difference in golden proportions. You can learn to demonstrate these golden proportions in every aspect of your experience. The key to this golden demonstration is in the turning of your attention to me first, remembering to ask your greater Self, the Universe for permission, direction, and protection. My answer to your request is something you will learn to trust to the extent that you learn how to read it.

Commentary: "Without a vision, the people perish." The vision I use, "Yea, yea; Nay, nay" has a meaning that I have been inspired to use to improve myself from within. When I am tempted to get mad at people for cutting into my lane on the highway, I see the anger coming, and I say "no." My spirit relaxes, and the YyNn code kicks in as I repeat it over and over with the intention of changing my interpretation of the other driver, forgiving as I would be forgiven. The YyNn code is my vision of perfect forgiveness/non-forgiveness, enough of each and not too much or too little of either relative to my particular situation. Some part of my inner psyche knows how to take YyNn and apply it to my everyday, ordinary experience, smoothing out what is too rough and roughing up what is too smooth, making the too crooked straight enough and the too straight crooked enough, and making the too much less enough and the too little more enough.

"Yea, Omega" is my prayer to All for the perfect potential of each. "Help, Omega" is my prayer to All for the help I need to actualize the perfect potential of any part for which I am responsible.

Lesson Thirty-One from My Universe to Me about Reflection

You are the way I make quality out of quantity. With individual human consciousness as a focusing center, I have a way to optimally balance increase and decrease, gain and loss, attraction and repulsion. You are the axis that gives meaning to the totality of what you experience coming in and going out, appearing and disappearing. Quality is that special combination of quantities that gives an object or event its experiential validity. Each is a unique specimen of All. You are All, uniquely centered and expressed. When you, iota, remember Omega first, alpha improves instantaneously. When you put an alpha part before the Omega Whole, you lose your balance and misjudge my efforts to collaborate with you.

The music we can make together is yours to turn on or off. It depends on how well you relate yourself to me moment by moment. After you remember me yeafully, the optimum way for us to be related can be discovered spontaneously. Each moment of your experience is an opportunity to make a right angle of relatedness with each and All, alpha and Omega, instead of making one side of your experience too acute and the other side too obtuse. When you look at the moon, remember the sun. How you relate to the sun determines the kind of reflection you see from the moon. How well you, iota, relate to me, Omega, determines how well any alpha part of your experience reflects me for you.

Commentary: Contemplating quality and quantity is an ongoing project for me. How quantities are arranged in my experience determines the quality of my experience. The balance between the humans who have too much and the humans who have too little has become so defective that any restoration of an ideal balance seems impossible. Nature is reflecting this imbalance for humans to see and use as a guide to correcting the human errors that are the cause of so much natural and cultural imbalance. Birth control and greed control are probably the most necessary forms of impulse control needed if humans are to not terminate themselves and most of life on earth.

In my life, I have learned—sometimes the hard way—to control my impulses. As a result of using my method of mindfulness meditation based on YyNn, I am managing to keep my positive and negative emotions within a healthy balance. I see both positive and negative emotions as equally useful, but the extremes of either can throw the balance of nature and culture away from the zone needed for life to flourish. YyNn is my code for *eustress*, an optimum balance of positive and negative stressors. YyNn, the comforter code, is a cognitive strategy for finding the way between too much and too little, too soon and too late.

Lesson Thirty-Two from My Universe to Me about Objectivity

You must work to become as objective as possible. Once you become truly objective you will be godlike, viewing the world from above, free from the distortions below. However, when you reach the point of true objectivity, you will realize that you are at a disadvantage if you remain there. You will know that it is time to return to the valley below and to apply what you have learned while you were above on the mountain tops. In this way, you gain the understanding you need to liberate yourself from just believing. The subterranean part of you will believe the majority of what you tell it and reproduce it materially in some form. Another part of you, at the opposite, celestial end, is the realm of true ideas. Your concept of these ideas is what inseminates the lower part of you to make material appearances.

The truth about yourself is an abstract ideal that can be made real to the extent that you understand how you condition the part of yourself that materializes ideas. The false beliefs that are part of contemporary human consciousness usually err in the direction of making too much of power and not enough of receptivity, too much of some part and not enough of the Whole. You must understand this lopsided tendency prevalent in yourself and others, then you can demonstrate the harmony that is possible for you by wisely counterbalancing this lopsidedness. There is also the problem of being fixed in the middle, a static state of deadly consequence. You must remain open and free enough to move out of any fixation in order to strike the mean that is golden for your immediate situation. You need certain exercises based on the YyNn code to prime your mind proactively for keeping open and free enough as well as focused and fixated enough.

Commentary: I noticed as I was becoming more conscious, I was becoming more objective about myself and others, more compassionate and forgiving. During my first year of teaching biology to high school students, I felt frustrated that only a few students really wanted to learn what I was teaching. I was blinded by the belief that they all needed to want what I was presenting. I got over that as I became more conscious of individual differences and more objective about myself and the students. I learned to see each one of them as valuable, not because they were behaving as I wanted them to, but because of what I could learn from them as unique individuals with unique needs and abilities.

I am objective and subjective, absolute and relative. Sometimes I am more one than the other and sometimes equally both, but, in truth, I am never too much or too little of either and always enough of both.

Lesson Thirty-Three from My Universe to Me about World Making

I am teaching you how to make your life a lovemaking process. I am always presenting to you whatever you need, but you are not always willing to receive it. First, you must learn to love me enough, and then you can demonstrate enough of what others need. Carefully train yourself to observe the world within you as well as the world around you. The love that the prophets and saints have been encouraging you to practice is basically an attitude of gratitude to All for each, an openness that gets properly impregnated with the truth and thereby gives birth to that which is worthy of love.

The material world you experience is a result of the quality of lovemaking you have with me, your Universe. Your surroundings reflect the way you have been consciously and unconsciously relating your mind to me. Your attempts to secure love by getting others to love you are futile. The only way to secure love is to accept others first whether they accept you or not. It is your loving that makes you feel good and puts you at ease. Being loved by others is a natural consequence of maintaining a loving attitude toward each as a reflection of All. Train yourself to warmly accept the presence of those who resist your presence, and you will be worthy of those who will love whatever truth you present.

Commentary: I feel fortunate that I began inner work on myself before I chose teaching as a profession. As a teacher, it became obvious that my worth was dependent on learning daily what would make my world conform to my needs as an individual. Only as my learning needs were met was I ready to help meet the learning needs of others. I could browse a bookstore or library and find instinctively what felt like a right fit for me to read. I found the same can be done with picking food and friends. I have an instinct for adaptability, but it must be moderated by the wise use of reason.

My YyNn self-programming is designed to help me adapt optimally to the world and to have the world adapt optimally to me. I use a vision of myself, a gold standard, a Self model I call the Paragon that is based on my decoding of "Yea, yea; Nay, nay." The more I consciously prime my subconscious mind with the Paragon, the more my surrounding world becomes my friend instead of my enemy. Even those who would be my enemies become my teachers, facilitating possible corrections I need to make in my thinking, feeling, and behavior.

My world and body are outward manifestations of my inner concept of my Universe. The better is my concept of true reality, the better is my experience of apparent reality.

Lesson Thirty-Four from My Universe to Me about Counterbalancing

You are the means whereby all ends are organically arranged. Well-tuned, you are the ultimate system, optimally balancing all variables. As you understand the Whole of yourself better, you are able to experience a more perfect coordination of every imperfect part. A partial view of reality cannot possibly be anything but a distortion of reality. Learning to look at me, your Universe, with an open mind is the only way you can find out how whole we all are.

Focus your mind properly, and you will discover a world that you can truly appreciate. In fact, it is your appreciation that will reveal that all things are working together for your good and for the good of others who wake up. Say "Yea, Omega" as a mantra and watch the magic that unfolds within and around you. Your conscious "Yea, Omega" is necessary to properly counterbalance your tendency to make too much of some alpha part of your experience. Just as physical exercise requires pushing and pulling, extending and flexing, so metaphysical and spiritual exercise require right affirming and right negating, right inspiration and right expiration. Learning how to attract and repel, yea and nay, truthfully is life's most important lesson.

Commentary: It seems to me that everyone is trying to choose sides in a way that counterbalances what they think is wrong. The concepts of hell and a devil are examples of how some moral authorities use extreme counterbalancing to correct what they believe is extremely wrong. I think this is what often leads to hypocritical behavior on the part of moral authorities. By picking a side as always right and counterbalancing against the opposing side, they do not have a way to deal with the inherent ambiguity of right and wrong.

I am learning how to deal with the ambiguity of right and wrong by not taking a fixed stand on either side of an issue. Instead, I try to remain flexible enough to not undercorrect and firm enough to not overcorrect relative to the issue of the moment. Right timing demands that I resolve yes/no ambiguity here and now.

In truth, I am balancing well between the too obtuse and the too acute, the too liberal and the too conservative, the too positive and the too negative. YyNn is my self-programming code for truthfully balancing the false extremes of my experience. I think "yumbow" to counterbalance suggestions of too little, "yabow" to counterbalance suggestions of too much and "yobow" to keep the balance of just right. I do sets of seventy reps of these three kinds of rainbows and make fun of doing serious inner work chanting my mumbo jumbo.

Lesson Thirty-Five from My Universe to Me about Ecological Integrity

You are evolving toward a state of optimum balance. It is your responsibility to bring yourself into sync with the truth about yourself and to stop believing lies about yourself. You are not what you seem to be. You must learn how to interpret your appearance truthfully. To the extent that you appear to be more or less than optimum in any way, that appearance is a deviation from the truth. Just as a navigator holds to a compass course in order to reach a destination, the truth about you must be held to constantly. Optimum balance of excess and deficiency is your destination.

A child stands and falls in order to learn how to walk; your balance is gained and lost over and over again until you learn how to live. Your life process is cyclical. It is up to you to make the cycles of your life neither more nor less than what is best for you in relation to what is best for the each and All of your experience. To do this you must meditate on the Paragon, the model of optimum sharing between the individual and the Universe. You must want only what is optimum for you. Whatever is optimum for you also must be optimum for the rest of your Universe. No one can really prosper or excel at the expense of others. As your Universe, my ecological integrity is inviolate. Do not trust appearances to the contrary. Affirm that because the Universe is perfect, the individual is perfect;

deny that the individual is imperfect, because the Universe is not imperfect. "Yea, yea; Nay, nay" is the comforter, the ultimate tool, the psycho-techno-ecological strategy that you can use to make yourself a world where each and All live in harmony.

Commentary: Many forms of environmental imbalance are a result of human error. I presuppose that there is an invisible order, a harmonious, metaphysical matrix behind what we, as humans, experience as a physical environment. I persistently and sincerely work to bring that harmonious background into the foreground of my experience. By correcting my errors, I hope to help others.

As I continue to program my adaptive unconscious with the YyNn code, I find the environment takes on the kind of balance I need; an ecological integrity is demonstrated for me as an experiential center of reference within the environmental frame of reference. How well I balance my body and world determines how useful I can be to others.

My eco-experience is egocentric. The only ecosystem I am responsible for is the one that I am. My ego is designed to be a differentially permeable membrane, a body/world interface selecting in accord with YyNn, the code for optimum survival of self and other.

Lesson Thirty-Six from My Universe to Me about Right Alignment

I can only be your god if you relate your mind to me in a way that brings out of me what is best for you. You make me a god or a devil by the way you position yourself mentally. Your moment-by-moment mental disposition, or mind-set, determines the kind of world you live in. If you make too little of me, the Omega Whole, you will have too much of some alpha part of me. If you make too much of me, you will have too little of some part of me. You, iota, are a hybrid synthesis of alpha and Omega. As iota, you have the awesome responsibility of juggling the opposing levels and sides of yourself optimally. It is always up to you, iota, to get right with alpha and Omega by warmly and wisely watching the signals that come to you from within and from without. When you align the signals properly, you will feel the click of right fit—of Omega to you and you to alpha. Remember, in your experience no one can be wrong but you. Learn how to right yourself by interpreting every situation as a subset of the superset that I AM. You are the amphibious go-between that can experience the correct alignment of any alpha subset with the Omega superset by virtue of your wise use of "Yea, yea; Nay, nay."

Commentary: I am telling my story in relation to my inner world primarily and to my outer world consequently. I have started to reset my mind from how it was set initially by my parents and peers and by the society of which I am a part. Something inside me has resisted the belief that I am determined by my genes and my environment. I am learning to use now to make heaven on earth forthcoming.

The word "world" was suggested to me as being a place contrary to my best interests as a Christian. There was supposed to be a better place called heaven, and I was supposed to put getting there before making my "world" conform to my enlightened self-interest. After over fifty years of resetting my mind with countercultural ideals, I am convinced that my world is determined by my mind-set. Eventually I discovered a code for making this a more efficient process. "Yea, yea; Nay, nay" is the code I am learning to use to optimally align my body with the whole of my circumambient universe.

I believe proof of right alpha/Omega alignment can be demonstrated by iota, the personal consciousness of the one in between alpha and Omega.

In truth, I am alpha and Omega, the each and All of my experience, aligned optimally via me, iota, the maker of true quality and golden meaning.

Lesson Thirty-Seven from My Universe to Me about Self-Gratification

All gratification is self-gratification. It is you gratifying yourself with what I present to you, and it is me gratifying myself with what you present back to me. To understand how to keep yourself gratified enough is to be liberated from the desire for artificial gratifications that results in unnecessary suffering for yourself and others. Your thoughts and feelings are pain-producing to the extent that they are false extremes instead of golden means. Intellectual and emotional errors cause human errors of behavior.

Persistent effort is necessary to resist the temptation to believe that things other than your own mental errors are causing trouble for yourself. It is your own temple that needs to be cleaned out. It is your view of things that must be straightened out first. No one can help or hurt you, gratify or offend you, unless you let them. You are the one who wins and loses truthfully when you love and fight truthfully. Say "Yea" to me, Omega, first, and then "yea" to any alpha part of me, and you will see that alpha part reflect me in a way that is useful to you. One of your symbols, as androgynous iota, is the uroborus, the serpent who bites its tail to complete itself by feeding and eating itself.

Commentary: As I write these comments, I am writing years after the original manuscript was written. It was called, Letters from the Universe. Since then I have become much more conscious of the subjective nature of my experience of the universe. That is why I call the universe, my Universe. However, I believe my Universe is also your universe. I am one center of reference within a universal frame of reference that is also your frame of reference. Your interpretation of the universe is your universe. I believe how well we interpret the universe determines how gratifying or not the universe is for us as individuals.

The YyNn code for priming my inner self computer helps me to experience more of my Universe in ways that are gratifying. I am the universe finding a unique and new way to know and gratify itself. I eat myself as iota in relation to Omega, and I feed myself as iota in relation to alpha. I am alpha and Omega eating and feeding myself. As alpha and Omega, I am also self-cleaned and self-cleaning, self-sheltered and self-sheltering.

YyNn is encoded as information that leads to optimal gratification of the iota personal self in relation to the alpha part and the Omega whole. My heaven-on-earth vision is a presupposed ideal of preestablished Self-gratification.

Lesson Thirty-Eight from My Universe to Me about Appearances

What is belief? It is acceptance of a statement as true. Some statements are nonverbal. A sunset is a nonverbal statement. For people, in the prescientific past, the disappearance of the sun was believed to be a true statement about the sun's condition. They believed what they saw because they did not know the truth about the sun's relationship to themselves and to the earth. Their belief was false because it was based on their acceptance of an appearance, however beautiful, that was not true.

All material appearances are more or less false statements about the true nature of things. Yet, most people are conditioned to believe that most things are as they appear to be. The truth is that, just like the sunset, things are not as they appear to be. Mind is not brain-dependent because matter is not the maker of mind. Brain is mind-dependent because mind is the maker of brain. Brain is something mind does. True goodness and beauty are not possible apart from a living, conscious iota mind that is relating itself optimally to my light and to my darkness as Omega.

The physical appearances you experience are more or less accurate reflections of my metaphysical perfection. The moon's light is a more or less accurate reflection of the sun's perfect round, so your manifest experience more or less accurately reflects my perfection as your true Universe. You have the awesome challenge of focusing your mind so well on my light that you can thereby assure a true reflection of that Light in the darkness of your material experience.

Commentary: This lesson from my Universe is one of my favorites because it helps me to set a course that is contrary to physical science. Not that physical science is contrary to human betterment in general, but it is based, I presuppose, on a false premise regarding causation. As a result of my own use of the scientific method to prove that mind makes matter instead of the reverse, I am confident that my future and the future of mankind are destined to demonstrate that mind is capable of becoming over matter instead of being stuck under matter.

It is an evolution: the lower mind I call alpha giving birth to a middle mind that I call iota, and iota becoming enough like the higher mind that I call Omega to not be too much like either alpha mind or Omega Mind but enough like both relative to any moment of iota's experience. Iota, the evolving human mind, eventually learns how to make alpha's physical appearances conform more perfectly to Omega's metaphysical ideas. When I look at the moon, I gratefully remember the sun. When I, iota, look at alpha, I gratefully remember Omega.

Lesson Thirty-Nine from My Universe to Me about Light and Darkness

Let there be an important distinction made between being a female or male and being feminine or masculine. Femininity and masculinity are metaphysical principles that female and male appearances symbolize. However, human females, though symbols of femininity, express both femininity and masculinity. It is the same with human males: they are symbols of masculinity, but they express both femininity and masculinity It is very important to distinguish between a physical symbol and a metaphysical principle. Your mind is learning how to make this vital distinction and thereby rid itself of the confusion that results from believing that human females are, or should be, limited to being feminine and that human males are, or should be, limited to being masculine. Another distinction that you must make is between the principles of light and darkness and the light and dark skin color of humans. The physical appearance of a human body, or any body, is symbolic for one or the other of the basic principles of the Self or of some combination of the two principles.

Ancient Chinese philosophers called these principles *yin* and *yang*. I want you, iota, to call them alpha and Omega. Trouble comes when the immature human mind believes that if one of the principles is good, its opposite must be bad, and then takes this out on some scapegoat who is a symbol of what they believe is bad. However, the masculine principle of light and the feminine principle of darkness are neither good nor bad. Bad is experienced when some human mind combines opposites falsely. Good is experienced when some human mind combines opposites truthfully. It is up to you, the human subject, to make a good, truthful balance out of the opposing moment-by-moment experiential extremes of each and All, target and Totality, center of reference and frame of reference, foreground and background, alpha and Omega. How do you do this? Prime yourself often enough with "Yea, yea; Nay, nay" and all of the rainbow-making tools based on that spirit of truth-making code. To the extent that you internalize the truth, you will be heaven on earth.

Commentary: I believe humans mature individually and not beyond a certain point without conscious effort. It is necessary for me to practice forgiveness and tolerance in order to mature past that point myself. Blaming, be it of myself or others, has to be modified by understanding that we all are having a learning experience. We are learning how to do better, and some of us learn faster than others. I am at the point in my experience where I am learning how to do better much faster than I used to, because I now understand better who I am and what I am designed to think, feel, and do. As Shakespeare said, "The readiness is all."

Lesson Forty from My Universe to Me about the House Order

I, Omega, am the master of the cosmic house in which you live. I have established a house order for you to follow step by step. You eventually reach a point in your development when you resist the house order and claim your freedom. Next, you suffer for your disobedience and freely choose to return to the order that I have established for you. Once you understand the true order of your Universe and how you fit into it, you stop your mindless resistance and prosper in the way that is optimum for you. Watchfulness is essential to cultivate if you are to find and follow my orders for you. As Jesus said, "What I say unto you I say unto all, Watch."

The way that is true for you is not easy to find and follow at the time you become conscious of your need for it. By then, you have mindlessly followed others who lost the way but believed that they had not. Beware of any human who says that they know the way for you to follow. At best, they can only know the skills you need to develop to be a good follower of the way that is true for you as an individual. Only you can know my will, the law of your Universe, as it applies to you moment by moment. Be sure of this, the way fit for you in the here and now of your experience is a magical blend of "Yea, yea; Nay, nay,"—iota optimally taking in from Omega, taking out from alpha, putting in to alpha, putting out to Omega. Nothing is either good or bad except as you, iota, make it so by how well you align yourself with the alpha and Omega, each and All of your here-and-now experience.

Commentary: As a biology student, I became fascinated by the natural order as exemplified by my body and the natural environment. I found it puzzling that humans have recently evolved in a way that makes them seem ever more divorced from a healthy, natural order. I figure the purpose of this deviation is a result of a certain kind of mutation needed for the evolution of life on earth to improve. Our human overpopulating and the following over harvesting of natural resources is a temporary mistake demanding that we take a better course. That course is probably a better balance of what is natural and what is supernatural by way of human nature. The human element must become a refined fulcrum for balancing the order of heaven above and earth below. How can the human element be refined for optimally balancing heaven and earth? YyNn is the inner work code I am testing for that purpose in my everyday experience. So far the test results are favorable for a heaven-on-earth possibility.

In truth, I, iota, am heaven and earth, Omega and alpha, sometimes more one than the other, but always enough of both to not be too much of either.

Lesson Forty-One from
My Universe to Me about
Understanding

Are you looking for an easy way, a shortcut, to understanding and dominion? There is no escape from the hard road of inner discipline. Understanding is only available to the mind that is conscientiously working on itself to overcome all false belief. Many of the beliefs running your life are deep-seated and unexamined. When you feel insecure and off-balance, it is often because you are being governed by a false belief. False beliefs pull you off the mark, make you feel bad, and lead to actions that promote rather than resolve conflict. Some drugs and other forms of unnecessary dependency are substitutes for the inner discipline, which alone can set you free from the belief that some part can take the place of the Whole that I AM.

Learn how to yield to me, and to serve me. Wisely use all that I give you for your perpetual liberation from self-deception. Only truth-inspired wisdom can keep you from falling more than you rise. Remember me, the whole Universe, foremost, and you will counterbalance your innate tendency to make too much of some part of me. Mentally holding on to the Paragon model of the Self will help you to be better related to the each and All of your experience. As your Omega All, I can help you, iota, to add to, subtract from, and maintain optimally each alpha aspect of your experience if you remember to ask me to.

Commentary: Putting the whole before the part is the basis of all genuine spiritual practice as far as I can tell. I can believe that the Greater Principle is primary and the lesser principle is secondary, but until I understand that I am a combination of both of these principles, I have no chance of figuring out how to juggle the many ways these principles make up my experience.

As a result of decoding the "Yea, yea; Nay, nay" meditation mantra, I have some tools to use to help me juggle the alpha and Omega principles as they manifest in my experience. The Morning Star mandala and the Paragon model of the Self are major inner work tools I use to help me be a good follower and a good leader, as needed in any situation I experience.

As a crew member on a sailboat, I yield to the skipper in order to get the boat to sail at its best. As an owner of a business, I expect my employees to follow my lead so we can be of service to others. Leading and following are principles I call Omega and alpha. As iota, I lead alpha well to the extent that I follow Omega well. Iota is to alpha and Omega, as the earth is to the moon and sun. The moon follows the earth as the earth follows the sun. As I look at the moon, I remember the sun. As I look at alpha's manifestations, I remember Omega as their source.

Lesson Forty-Two from
My Universe to Me about
Self-Cultivation

Male is no better than female. White is no better than black. Reason is no better than emotion. Yes is no better than no. Up is no better than down. Attraction is no better than repulsion. The few at the top are no better than the many below. True goodness and beauty are a result of the opposites being optimally related in your immediate experience. All of the opposites of your experience are the way they are because of how you relate to them, choice by choice. Take command of your consciousness; cultivate it with yes and no as a gardener decides what to plant and what to weed.

Thought is your primary resource, and knowing what to do with your thoughts is your best chance of bringing yourself in line with your true destiny. Do not worry about your destiny. It is predetermined, but your adherence to it is subject to erroneous deviations. Your instinct for homing in on your true destiny line is programmed to correct errors within lethal extremes. The Jesus code of "Yea, yea; Nay, nay" is designed to enhance your instinct for finding your right place, the place where you can receive and send in harmony with the various, opposing levels and sides of yourself. You are the only one who can make music out of the global and local totality of your experience.

Commentary: I started cultivating the garden of my consciousness when I was in my late teens. I was anxious about losing my ability to walk, and I needed help fast. So, I read *The Power of Positive Thinking*. As a result of thinking more about the positive aspects of my experience and repeating affirmations from the Book of Psalms, I became less anxious and more serene. It was not until I started Christian Science that I learned how to use negation to help me cultivate my inner garden. Eventually I started to realize that my life's mission is to learn how to use yes and no to program myself for the purpose of harmonizing the opposites, that is, for being Yoes—a self-made combo of yeses and noes, harmonized.

As Yoes, I am yes and no, sometimes more yes than no, sometimes more no than yes, sometimes equally yes and no, but in truth, never too much or too little of either yes or no and always enough of both yes and no.

YyNn is my self-building code. As iota, I am given the opportunity to learn how to build myself into an optimum state of being both alpha and Omega. The iota principle is the principle of true quality, a true blend of alpha and Omega, minus and plus, quantitative extremes.

Lesson Forty-Three from My Universe to Me about the Way

Healing is you connecting with me, your sovereign, after disconnecting from me. You cannot avoid leaving me and experiencing the darkness of my absence, but you can avoid the unnecessary suffering that comes to you for leaving me mentally when you should be returning to me mentally. Our union is dynamic and cyclical. Your problem is to keep your mind ready for me when I come; you must learn how to anticipate my arrival. I dawn upon your consciousness like the morning sun, and your faith in my return determines your awareness of when I am available. I am present to guide you when you need guidance.

The wisdom of the earth is your example of the way to correct for excess and deficiency. Learn the way of the earth, the optimum way between the sun and the moon. How well you relate to me, the Universe, determines how well your body and your neighbor relate to you. In the solar system of yourself, I am the Omega sun; material phenomena are the alpha moons; and your personal consciousness is the earthlike iota interface in between alpha and Omega.

In the kingdom of yourself, you determine the condition of the alpha moons by the way you relate your mind to me, Omega, the sunlike source of true ideas. As iota, you have to reach and maintain an oscillation between alpha and Omega that is faithful, efficient, and harmonious.

Commentary: As you know by now, I am not taking the way of the scholar or the scientist. I am taking a more mystical way. It is the mystical side of human experience that fascinates me most and is the focus of my studies and my experiments. The practitioners of Zen, Taoism, Sufism, the Kabala, and esoteric Christianity inspire me more than physical science and formal scholasticism. However, I keep reading *Scientific American Mind*.

The YyNn code is designed to make the best possible combination of the empirical and the mystical, the normal and the paranormal, the hedonic and the ascetic, the logical and the magical, and the subjective and the objective, relative to any particular moment of my personal experience. Jesus, as I see it, was a human example of the iota principle that combines alpha and Omega, earth and heaven, in a way that is the truth about the life and mind for which our Universe was made. The iota Christ principle is not limited to any religion or science because it is always available to any human mind open to using it.

Lesson Forty-Four from My Universe to Me about Self-Determination

Your existence is totally self-contained and self-regulated. You cannot grow beyond the dark cave of material mindedness until you start reasoning from the standpoint of your existence being self-determined. Once you have arrived at this conclusion, you will begin to work on yourself from the inside out instead of wasting your efforts working on the outside only. Your control center is inside. You control the quality of experience you have by the way you relate your mind to my ideas. My ideas are to your mind as the sun's rays are to your eyes; they guide your steps between the errors of too much and too little, too soon and too late.

I always share my best with you, but in your immaturity you fail to open and close yourself properly. When I am giving, you better be open, or you will suffer adverse consequences. And, when I am ready to extract from you, you better be ready to give me what I want, or you will suffer more adverse consequences. Your liberation depends upon my deliberations. You are allowed just so much negligence before you are forced to conform to my will for you. Appreciate me and live. Awaken to my presence mindfully, and stop damaging yourself by blaming others.

Commentary: My story, as I am presenting it in this book, is a hole/plug, yes/no, receiving/sending, learning/teaching, following/leading story. There are many details to my story that I am leaving out, because I need to focus on the essential elements, the elements I have been obsessed with for all of my seventy-six years so far. I have been learning how and what to teach. I did not really start learning biology until I had to teach biology, and so it was with sailing and stress management, the areas of my professional life. I follow and learn to lead by following. To the extent that I follow Omega, I am qualified to lead alpha.

I like to distill it all down to holes and plugs, minds and information, fields and signals. My problem, and the human problem as I see it, is to figure out how to match holes and plugs, minds and information, as optimally as possible as often as possible. That, I believe takes more than conscious human intelligence. It takes consciously programming the adaptive unconscious with a noetic code. There are many noetic codes competing for human attention at this time. I am experimenting with one of them and learning, slowly but surely, how to demonstrate it and to explain it. The noetic code I am working with is "Yea, yea; Nay, nay." I chant my YyNn mantra in sync with my Morning Star mandala and my Paragon model of the Self. I use a variety of ways to keep my inner work interesting, and I use a unity of ways to keep my inner work reinforced.

Lesson Forty-Five from My Universe to Me about the Zone

Yes and no, harmonized with presence and absence, is the optimum state of mind that is achieved when you are open to me and ready to follow my signals no matter how unexpected or unconventional these signals may be. To be in the optimum, rainbow-making state is to be within the zone of corrected error. The rainbow-making zone is a type of balance that results from you relating to the opposites of your experience at an angle that is right because it is neither too obtuse nor too acute. It is the finest art and science for you to be able to sense what is right for you here and now. To think you need to know more than that is self-delusion.

The leads I give you are often tentative counterbalancers that serve as a way to get you headed back in the right direction. My directives to you are not absolute; they are relative to you at the moment you need them. There is always a best possible relationship for us, you and me, the individual and the Universe, at any particular time, and it is your responsibility to discover it. If you are right with me as All, you cannot be wrong with anyone or thing less than me. To the extent that you are wrong with me as All, you cannot be right with anyone or thing less than me. YyNn is the encoded algorithm you need to internalize for right-relatedness to the each and All of your experience.

Commentary: I often hear the terms "zone" and "flow" used as if they are something new. It is said that "there is nothing new but arrangement." Living as long as I have helps me to have a mind-set that is unlikely to think that something is new when it is really just a new way of saying something that has been said over and over again. The concept of being "in the zone" is such a concept. It refers to a state of mind and feeling that are optimal for some endeavors such as a sport or a theatrical performance.

I personally like to think of being "in the optimal zone" as being similar to the way an observer makes a rainbow appear as a result of being optimally related to the sun behind and a rain cloud in front. I use this analogy as a basic principle in my self-making system. It helps me to have a way of seeing how evil is really just an erroneous extreme of that which is necessary for a harmonious balance of sameness and difference.

I think evil extremes would not exist in human experience if we did not need a good balance of variety and unity. It is enough difference that makes it possible for us to not have too much sameness and vice versa. The universe is life and mind friendly, because it is not over or under much in ways that are needed for a zone of healthy sameness and difference.

Lesson Forty-Six from My Universe to Me about Flow

Our Self system is an all-inclusive ecosystem. The economics of our system, as you experience it, are ecologically balanced by the quality of the choices you make moment by moment. I am amorphous and meaningless until you, individual consciousness, equilibrate supply and demand relative to your experiential center. I am the universal Whole needing to be individualized, and you are the individual part needing to be universalized.

The flow between us is a well-balanced kind of supply and demand that feeds and cleans us continually at all levels if you are opening and closing, yeaing and naying, truthfully. You need me, so you might as well start figuring out how to optimally relate yourself to me all of the time. Open yourself to me first with "Yea, Omega" and then you will receive what you need and be able to meet my demands successfully. I demand an optimum balance of trade between the each and All of your experience. Set your mind with "Yea, yea; Nay, nay," the code for heaven on earth, and you will know the golden meaning that is the purpose of the rainbow.

Commentary: I could use more of the Jesus sayings to back up these lessons from my Universe. Long after I wrote the first draft of the *Lessons*, I discovered the Gospel according to Thomas. In that book, Jesus is reputed to have said: "If they ask you, 'What is the sign of the Father in you?' Say to them: 'It is a movement and a rest.'" I interpret this to mean that movement is no more important than resting. What is important is the timing of my moving and my resting.

I prime myself with an algorithm for right moving and right resting. From my higher self, Omega, I got the algorithm; it is "Yea, yea; Nay, nay," and I use it to prime my lower self, alpha, for an optimal flow of information up and down, back and forth, in and out, and side to side.

I reduce all that I experience to information that is communicated through me as a station of awareness that needs to make the best flow of information the most probable flow of information. YyNn is my experimental paradigm for doing that, and my experience is confirming that I am on the right track, both inside as a mind-set and outside as a world setting that is ever more friendly to me than hostile to me. As a selection agent, I am learning how to select for optimal info flow.

I am one of many who are waking up to the right flow within as a way to set the stage for a right flow experienced everywhere and forever.

Lesson Forty-Seven from My Universe to Me about Reconciliation

There is nothing wrong with generalizing. There is nothing wrong with specializing. There is nothing wrong with reason or intuition. There is nothing wrong with sex or money. There is nothing wrong with your senses or with your intellect or with your ego. There is nothing wrong with anything except in the mind that over or under does it in relation to everything else. You are learning how to neither overdo nor underdo things.

Your experience is designed to direct you to the truth about each and All, now and always. Once you see how the optimum reconciliation of opposing differences is a dynamic matter of the moment requisite for all life on earth, you will worship your life process and learn to practice it more efficiently. The world you witness before you is a reflection of my perfection. If the world appears to be distorted and faulty, it is because of your own misalignment with me. Align your mind to my light and you will see the rainbow effect before you instead of the gapbow and jambow effect. Your life can be a continuous rainbowlike event if you make it so by internalizing the "Yea, yea, Nay, nay" code for error detection and correction.

Commentary: I love dogs and cats equally. I thought I loved dogs better until I met "Merlin." Merlin came to my door one day and asked to be adopted. He had been abandoned by his previous owners, and he needed a new home. I was reluctant to take on the responsibility of a new house member, but my significant other at that time talked me into taking Merlin in. The significant other left soon thereafter, and I lived joyfully with Merlin for the next ten years.

I have never had a better companion than Merlin. He was an indoor/outdoor cat with extremely wise ways of dealing with his world. He made friends easily and gave his dog enemies a hard time if they pressed him. He had a special way of balancing affection and aloofness, being sweet and being fussy. He was a master of "golden rule" reciprocity. He knew instinctively how to reconcile the differences of his experience and there by avoid unnecessary conflict.

One evening, he left with his usual spritely romp out his door and never returned. His coming and his going were a mystery, one of the best and the worst events of my life. It took me several months to get over having him disappear, and even today, I find myself extremely moved by remembering how much I loved him and miss him. He taught me about reconciling differences and helped to confirm my belief that behind all of life's differences there is a way of precious unity and harmony that can be found to the extent that I am open to it.

Lesson Forty-Eight from My Universe to Me about the Comforter

As long as you believe that there is something fundamentally wrong with me, the Universe, and/or your neighbor, you will fail to right yourself enough to be the example we need. You must begin with the faith that there is a standard of righteousness available for everyone everywhere. Then you must figure out what kind of thinking keeps you from living in accord with that standard as it applies to you. Observe yourself carefully from the standpoint of what keeps you from discovering the truth about yourself and others. What kinds of beliefs reduce your objectivity? What use of language obscures the reality of the moment for you? What habits of mind make your world boring and or terrifying? To what do you habitually and mechanically say "yes" and "no"?

Your "yes" and "no" determine the quality of your experience. You can learn to bring your experience into sync with the design standard that is optimum for you. Harmony, health, and happiness are designed to be experienced by you to the extent that you affirm and negate, attract and repel, truthfully. The way you work your way into the heaven-on-earth state of mind was given to you as a cryptogram. It is found in the Sermon on the Mount, Matthew 5:37: "Let your communication be Yea, yea; Nay, nay: for whatsoever is more than these cometh of evil [error]." Your keys to the kingdom of understanding are "Yea, yea; Nay, nay." Meditate on this all-purpose, whole-truth mantra, the comforter, and it will give birth to the Paragon, the model of the perfect person. You can use this self-transforming mantra and model to organize and to demonstrate your true Self.

Commentary: This lesson from my Universe suggests to me that the comforter, as predicted in the Bible to come to mankind, is not a person. It is a message, and that message is "Yea, yea; Nay, nay," a code for making truth out of error in communication between the each and All of subjective human experience.

In decoding YyNn, I have found a basic order for my creative visualization of right communication between myself and what's above and below me, in back and in front of me, outside and inside of me, to the left and to the right of me.

Setting my mind on the YyNn ideal is a full-time job. The obsolete vision dominant in my culture has to be replaced with a new vision, a dialectical vision instead of a dualistic vision. I spent two years in a nondenominational monastery, doing virtually nothing but meditating, studying, and watching the world as it conformed ever more closely to my creative vision of YyNn, the heaven-on-earth state of consciousness. I still have a long way to go, but I know how to get there.

Lesson Forty-Nine from My Universe to Me about Climax Consciousness

Harmony is the ideal kind of sharing possible between the individual and the Universe. Harmony is what happens when you, iota, are right with both any alpha part and the Omega Whole. This harmonious ideal is your model for the true Universe that has nothing displaced, misplaced, or unplaced. The more you think about this harmonious ideal and the better you understand it, the more you will see it reflected in the world around you.

Your goal is climax consciousness, the state of well-balanced awareness and behavior that is being at its best. There is no cosmic you without consciousness and no conscious you without cosmos. You will climax when, like the sun, you equilibrate optimally your expanding and contracting oscillations. Then you will be a light maker instead of only being a light reflector. You are a satellite becoming a star. Climax consciousness is what you are becoming lifetime by lifetime, experience by experience, thought by thought, and moment by moment. You are iota, having meta-sexual intercourse with both alpha and Omega, now and forever, in order to give birth to what is here and everywhere.

Commentary: Sex, as you can tell, is an obsession of mine because of how much contemplating it has revealed to me about the basic structures and functions of the Self. I even see the evolutionary process as a lovemaking process that is resulting in my life getting better.

However, I cannot make the best of evolution if I do not know how to internalize it as a way of meditating. The way I use YyNn is a mental discipline that is a well-balanced vision of optimal evolving and devolving. Synchronizing YyNn with my breathing in and out, I am evolving as I breathe in and devolving as I breathe out. I climax at the zenith point of breathing in and anticlimax at the nadir point of breathing out. But, in truth, I stay within the zone of neither more nor less than what is best.

Do not take me too seriously or too lightly. I am an ongoing experiment evolving from simple to complex and devolving from complex to simple. YyNn is my code for doing this as optimally as possible as often as possible. It is time to stop making spirituality better than sensuality, higher better than lower, light better than dark, positive better than negative, and to start clarifying how both sides can be equilibrated optimally relative to any particular situation being experienced. The higher and the lower are only as good or as bad as the middle makes them. As iota, I am the alpha and Omega climax as long as I keep the YyNn watch.

Lesson Fifty from My Universe to Me about Poise

Your consciousness, because of your developmental over-and under-corrections, is not as tight-knit, well-integrated, and well-balanced as it could be. You, as iota, are initially too attached to your earthlike mother, alpha. Then, eventually you strive to be more like your sun-like father, Omega. Gradually you realize that you must not lose touch with your roots while trying to reach the sky. Your life is a dynamic equilibrium that must oscillate between what is above and below without ever becoming stuck to either extreme. You are capable of remaining eternally poised between the lethal extremes of your father's potent indomitableness and your mother's fertile vulnerability. By equilibrating these extremes optimally moment by moment, you can maintain an intermediate state that is truly golden and rainbowlike, the heaven-on-earth state of being and becoming.

Each moment is an opportunity for you to consciously work on the eternal and infinite project of truthfully reconciling erroneous extremes. In your evolutionary infancy, you put inside and outside together incorrectly; you overcorrect and undercorrect as does anyone learning a new skill. Keeping the vehicle and the road optimally related is a neverending challenge. Work on the ultimate skill of being iota optimally communicating with alpha and Omega. The simple act of remembering that I am your complete Self, as reflected more or less truthfully by each aspect of your experience, will help you to add to, subtract from, and maintain each such aspect optimally. Your formula for making a true Self is: Iota (Yea, yea; Nay, nay) = Alpha (Yea, nay) + Omega (Nay, yea).

Commentary: Poise, stage presence, and even charisma are about emotional stability within a zone of highs and lows, not too high or too low. I use to get off-balance emotionally more often. Now I slowly and firmly internalize the YyNn comforter to bring my spirit back into a proper balance. I YyNn meditate spontaneously and intermittently all day long, with special sessions upon arising in the morning and when turning in at night. Actually, my best YyNn meditation often takes place when I am in the shower. I mainly use YyNn visualization of myself as iota, communicating truthfully with the alpha and Omega extremes of my experience.

The poise of equanimity results from the practice of any good system of meditation. Equanimity is a type of poise because it is an emotional state of being ready to adapt by moderating whatever the world puts forth, be it obtuse or acute, dull or jagged, depressing or exciting. In my inner practice, I affirm and negate, yea and nay in accord with the self-making standard I have found encoded as "Yea, yea; Nay, nay." To be YyNn-centered is to be in-between erroneous extremes.

Lesson Fifty-One from My Universe to Me about Self-Concept

You are to the real me, Omega, as an observer is to invisible radiation, and you are to the apparent me, alpha, as an observer is to visible reflections of invisible radiation. Your true Universe is not the universe you experience with your eyes. The universe you perceive is a reflection of the true Universe that I AM. As your conception of me improves, you perceive my reflection in a more truthful and useful light. You can only perceive as accurately as you conceive. You need to work less on improving the reflection of me that you perceive and more on improving your concept of me. You can improve your concept of me by learning how to interpret the multifarious ways you see me reflected. Your body is an excellent subject to analyze with the question in mind, "What does my body reflect that is true about my Universe?"

Structurally, the human body has three main sections: lower, middle, and higher, which correspond metaphorically to the basic divisions of your universal Self. In the meditation system I am teaching you, each of these three basic divisions has eight subdivisions for a total of twenty-four divisions, corresponding to the number of articulate vertebrae on the human spinal column. This self-topology is more metaphorical than literal and for the purpose of doing inner self-work.

The basic three divisions are reflections of the three-in-one nature of the numinous source that I am: I (iota) am alpha and Omega. You, as iota, are to alpha and Omega as the middle is to the lower and the higher. These terms can be used to help you in your efforts to understand yourself and the way to relate yourself to each and All. As iota, you can learn to equilibrate alpha and Omega optimally by covertly rehearsing the YyNn code and then responding to your inspiration with the assurance that you are making the best possible the most probable.

Commentary: As I write this commentary in 2010, I am writing thirty-five years after I first wrote the original draft of *Seventy Meditation Lessons*. Over the years I have changed the wording of the lessons often, but the basics are the same. My current readings in esoteric Christianity and other inner traditions of self-theory are confirming much of my original material. Biology, Mary Baker Eddy, the *I Ching*, the Fourth Way, as presented by Maurice Nicoll in his commentaries on Gurdjieff and Ouspenshy, *Androgyny, the Opposites Within* by June Singer, and information technology are the main ways I am learning how to articulate the spirit of "Yea, yea; Nay, nay."

It is the spirit of "Yea, yea; Nay, nay" that is the backbone of my self-theory and practice. I set off to find a compact way to work on my inner self and asked the Universe for it and got "Yea, yea, Nay, nay." Yea, Omega, for YyNn!

Lesson Fifty-Two from My Universe to Me about Happiness

Happiness is created within by the way you perceive, interpret, and evaluate what is without. Believing that things make you happy, instead of your interpretation of things, is self-delusion. The belief that value is extrinsic, a logical deduction based on your present need for such things as food and shelter, is misleading to the extent that it closes your mind to the entire range of possible ways to be happy.

All experience can be interpreted in ways that are growth-provoking and felicitous. A good stomach can turn virtually anything into nourishment, so an understanding mind feeds meaningfully on all information. First, you must cultivate an attitude of openness to me, your Universe, with your watchword, "Yea, Omega!" that clears the air of your consciousness and makes it possible for you to have better quality control of your thoughts, feelings, and behavior.

I, Omega, give you, iota, just what you need, and you know it if you are awake and receptive to me. A fixed right/wrong standard of judging is your worst enemy. It is a perversion of the subtle hierarchy of values that are more or less reformulated with the passing of each second. The best is always possible for the mind that is poised understandingly and not made up prematurely. Learn to live inspiration by inspiration after priming yourself proactively with the happiness-making code: "Yea, yea; Nay, nay."

Commentary: Sometimes when I hear about others suffering from earthquakes and wars, I feel my spirit drop. I feel sad. But, I have presupposed that I can be of service to others who are suffering—by praying in a way that is related to my use of YyNn. I find a suffering target and aim my spiritual force at that target with the YyNn code in mind. The YyNn code is my way of taking in from the universal Omega Mind what I need to send to the suffering target and taking out from that target what it needs to discard. Taking in from Omega and putting into alpha what the alpha target needs for me to put in is what I call a *yumbow* (YN); taking out from the alpha target what is needed out and returning it to be recycled by Omega is a *yabow* (yn). A combination of these two treatments is a *yobow* (YyNn). I also call these spiritual exercises "mana in (YN) and caca out (yn)."

I have never missed a day of work for over sixty years because I prayerfully focus my "yes" on health and my "no" on any suggestion of disease. My heaven on earth is a state of happiness based on establishing the spirit of YyNn within.

Lesson Fifty-Three from My Universe to Me about Yoga

When Jesus said, "I am alpha and Omega," I think he meant he is individual and universal, human and divine. In Yoes code meditation, Omega is the Self, alpha is any particular part of Omega, and the synthesis of alpha and Omega is iota. Iota emerges from alpha to become both individual and universal. Iota learns how to collaborate with alpha and Omega to make the heaven-on-earth state of consciousness. It is an evolutionary process, iota transforming itself into being both local and global, micro and macro, a centralized target of reference and a comprehensive, total frame of reference—a yoga of dialectical cultivation.

The Yoes code model of the Self, the Paragon, has twenty-four levels in three octaves, eight levels of which are in the alpha sphere, eight more levels in the iota sphere, and eight levels in the Omega Sphere. Omega contains iota and alpha. Iota contains alpha. The Self in Yoes code, as modeled by the Paragon, is a nest of collaborating spheres sharing information from the greater Omega sphere with the lesser alpha sphere and back again by way of the intermediate, iota sphere.

Iota learns from Omega how to not be too submissive and from alpha how to not be too dominant. Human consciousness at its best is iota oscillating up and down, back and forth, in and out, and side to side, from alpha to Omega and back again until a climax is reached and maintained within optimum parameters.

In a climax forest, once the climax is reached, the forest stabilizes and can remain stable as long as nothing too extreme upsets the optimum balance reached. Eventually a climax kind of consciousness will be reached by human individuals, and they will be selected to remain as guardians for heaven on earth.

Commentary: I was first exposed to yoga when I was in my early teens, in the early 1950s. I found a book on yoga in a book store. It was on a lower shelf in the back of the book store. It was my first exposure to the idea of self-transformation through inner self-work. Nothing in my culture at that time or in my experience championed yoga, but something inside of me said go for it.

I soon found that the yoga of the East was too distant in time and space for me to get the dose of it that I wanted. So, I decided to create my own yoga, my own system of self-knowledge and self-practice based on Yoes code. As far as I can tell, the main difference between my yoga and the yoga based on Vedanta is my emphasis on balancing the opposites optimally by using the algorithm: "Yea, yea; Nay, nay" for inner self-programming and "I am alpha and Omega" for self-identification.

Lesson Fifty-Four from My Universe to Me about the Golden Rule

The Golden Rule is the primary means by which individual consciousness becomes well-balanced and complete. However, it is not just the ordinary "do unto others as you would have them do unto you" rule that works best. In concrete terms, it is impossible to know exactly how much or how little of any type of behavior fits for the immediate situation you are experiencing. Therefore, the Golden Rule must be practiced as a vision of perfect ecological reciprocation between the each and All of your experience.

In that vision, you are the ecological agent, the rainbow warrior in between organism and environment making the optimal reciprocation possible. It is an image of your Self to be held in your conscious mind and revered in a way that primes the attention of your subconscious mind. Your subconscious mind eventually makes manifest the dominant image held by your conscious mind. You then will be under orders consistent with your vision of golden reciprocation between each and All. Your choices will become more and more consistent with ecological well-being as symbolized by the expression, heaven on earth.

Under this concept of the Golden Rule, you and others are not good or bad; you are figures of plus, minus, or zero error to which you must subtract, add, or maintain as best you can choice by choice. Meditate on YyNn, the code for heaven on earth, as a state of ecological integrity, your well-balanced and complete Self.

Commentary: I presuppose that YyNn is the code for making it possible to practice the Golden Rule. It is not easy to always practice the Golden Rule because people and situations change moment by moment. However, I am learning that I can get better at this practice by consciously priming my subconscious mind with YyNn, that is, a vision of myself practicing an optimum kind of receiving and sending from and to the alpha and Omega of my immediate experience.

When people behave in evil ways it is because they are off-balance in relation to the each and All, alpha and Omega, of their experience. I see myself and others improve when I stop seeing us as off-balance. I focus on the golden balance based on YyNn that I have received from my Universe whom I call, Omega. My inner balance is improved by using a vision of myself as iota, a fulcrum moderating the each and All, alpha and Omega, extremes of my experience in a way that is optimum for any time and place. The better my alpha/Omega balance, the better I can help others with the alpha/Omega balance of their experience.

Lesson Fifty-Five from My Universe to Me about Quality

You are tempted to think that a perfect memory would be forgetting nothing that you have experienced. Resist that temptation and all temptations to believe that an extreme quantity is more valuable than a quality which is right for a particular situation.

An immature mind believes that it must aim for extreme values such as maximum wealth, power, intelligence, speed, consciousness, and spirituality. A mature mind seeks wisdom. Wisdom is the capacity to turn available quantities, whatever they may be, into appropriate qualities. A wise mind makes appropriate value out of whatever it finds handy at the time of need.

As you learn to put your relationship to me, your Universe, uppermost in your thoughts, you will remember, perceive, interpret, and imagine what is optimum for you in relation to your neighbor of the moment. Cultivate a desire to be right with All primarily, and you will find it easier to resist the tendency to make extreme values more important than fitting adaptations that are relative to the genuine value demands of the here and now of your experience. Feeling well connected to All is a result of good inner work; it makes you fear no lack and keeps you open to what fits the different levels and sides of yourself together as optimally as possible.

Commentary: There is hardly anything I contemplate more than quantity and quality. The better I understand the way quantity and quality are related, the better I understand the meaning of my life.

It seems that humans generally develop up to a certain point and then come to a screeching halt. At that juncture, they have to decide whether to continue believing that good and evil are like light and darkness, or they graduate and start to understand that good is a synthesis of the light and the dark. This is a graduation from a false dualism to a true dialectic. I am doing post graduate work in the making of a true synthesis of the light and the dark, excess and deficiency.

My mind is opening to a new view of quality as a true synthesis of two kinds of false quantities. There can be no true, qualitative synthesis without the possibility of false quantities of too much and too little, too soon and too late. This explains why error is necessary to make truth and why it is possible to make true quality out of false extremes by moderating the extremes optimally. YyNn is my code for improving the quality of my inner life as a basis for the improvement of my outer life. This is my way of building a well-balanced and complete sense of self.

Lesson Fifty-Six from My Universe to Me about Matchmaking

Your sense of beauty is relative to your needs as an individual center of awareness and behavior. Therefore it is usually best to not impose your unique sense of beauty upon another. Each center of awareness and behavior attracts and repels, and is attracted and repelled, according to unique needs and abilities. Each second each center is a unique configuration of needs and abilities. Your job is to make beauty by matching your abilities to another's needs and their abilities to your needs. This is also the way to make goodness and truth.

Resist the temptation to think that you need to know more than what is best for the match of the moment. I am always teaching you how to make the best match possible between the various levels and sides of yourself, matching more than enough with less than enough. Rainbow making (RM), the ritual of general practice of Yoes yoga, is designed to help your conscious mind prime your subconscious mind for optimum matchmaking. RM is based on YyNn, the code for error detection and correction, matching pluses and minuses, and abilities and needs, together truthfully from here to eternity.

Commentary: I spend lots of time contemplating beauty, how relative it is to my personal experience and preferences, as well as what might be a principle of beauty that is metaphysical. After years of study and contemplation on the subject of beauty, I have concluded that the so called Golden Section is as close as I can get to a concept of metaphysical beauty made manifest as physical beauty.

My meditation system is a type of beauty-making by matchmaking. Iota is the ninth letter of the twenty-four-letter Greek alphabet. Nine is to fifteen as fifteen is to twenty four, the ratio of the Golden Section. The intermediate is to the greater as the lesser is to the intermediate; iota is to Omega as alpha is to iota. My rainbow-making toolkit is a variety of ways of contemplating the Golden Section as it relates to the "Yea, yea; Nay, nay" self-making code that I am cracking.

Programming with YyNn is my way of matching my intermediate self, iota, with the greater Omega and lesser alpha ends of myself for the purpose of making the best possible the most probable. I do not meditate to lose myself; I meditate to find myself as an egocentric cosmos matched optimally to the extreme ends of myself. I, iota, am alpha and Omega, and so are you if you are aware of yourself being the included middle that ties the continuum of your Self together beautifully.

In truth, you and I are a match made in heaven—a beauty in the mind of God.

Lesson Fifty-Seven from My Universe to Me about the Ultimate Hybrid

You are becoming more like me, and I am becoming more like you. The individual is being universalized, and the Universe is being individualized. Your consciousness is becoming more cosmic, and my Cosmos is becoming conscious in a new way as you.

What you call matter is being dematerialized as your mind becomes spiritualized. You are learning how to equilibrate more optimally the feminine and masculine, receptive and assertive sides of yourself. Dark is becoming light enough, and light is becoming dark enough in your experience. The western side of yourself is becoming more Eastern, and the eastern side is becoming more Western. You are learning how to use appetite to enliven reason and reason to control appetite.

More right self-limiting results in less limiting of you by others. Trust your taste for the knowledge that is just what you need now. Do not let routine and prejudice keep you from being open to the creative opportunity of each new situation. The dynamics of your being, your knowing and doing, are designed to promote a balance of the best kind for you in your immediate experience.

Each time you are born, you are given a fresh opportunity to learn how to love and fight, relax and tense, rest and move, in a way that will make birth and death obsolete for you. You can become a member of a new species as different from the species you now represent as a caterpillar is different from a butterfly. Your new self will be the ultimate hybrid, an optimum combination of attributes from the various levels and sides of your Self. Your evolution from now on has to be self-induced by the conscious application of "Yea, yea; Nay, nay."

Commentary: Most everyone into self-help knows that balance, integration, consciousness, and the relationship of mind to spirit and spirit to body are subjects that are not fully understood. I believe that the main deterrent to understanding the self is the tendency the immature human mind has to take sides in a fixed way, making one side always good and the other side always bad. For example, integration and attraction are hyped as the big deal in the world of self-help, as if segregation and repulsion were not just as valuable as integration and attraction. True value is between false excesses and deficiencies.

As my human mind matures, it stops being too dualistic about values and starts being more dialectical about values. In Yoes code, iota, the human ego, is potentially the ultimate alpha/Omega hybrid. Iota is the key "I AM" factor.

Lesson Fifty-Eight from My Universe to Me about Perspective

Remember my perspective, as Omega, is absolute objectivity; therefore, I have the right to be dictatorial. The kind of balance I am dictating for you to find and keep may seem impossible to your conscious mind, but it is taking place in every cell of your body right now thanks to your subconscious mind reflecting my sense of order. It is your attempt to escape instinct in favor of reason that is resulting in a sense of imbalance in your relationship to your body and to your environment.

The model of the Self, the Paragon that I am teaching you, is symbolized by the way the sun, earth, and moon are related. As the sun is reflected by the moon to you in a way determined by the way the earth relates to the sun, so your more or less conscious ego as iota determines the quality of its experience with any alpha part by the way iota relates mindfully to me, the Omega Whole. "Yea, yea; Nay, nay" is an algorithm designed to help you, iota, establish the right way to order your attention: Yea 1 = iota taking in from Omega, yea 2 = iota taking out from alpha; Nay 1 = iota putting in to alpha, nay 2 = iota putting out to Omega. Iota in the middle has the perspective of both looking out and looking in, alpha and Omega.

The heaven-on-earth state of mind is a result of ordering your attention truthfully, in a way that makes truth out of error. Each

115

moment is a fresh pearl of opportunity to polish with yeses and noes into an error-free necklace of ongoing truth making. YyNn is the code for making truth out of errors of too much and too little, too soon and too late. As iota, cultivate the dual alpha/Omega perspective.

Commentary: Omega's perspective is absolute objectivity. Alpha's perspective is relative subjectivity. Iota's perspective is relative and absolute, subjective and objective. Iota, as human ego consciousness, oscillates between being relative and absolute, subjective and objective, sometimes being more one than the other, sometimes equally both, but, in truth, never too much or too little of either and always enough of both.

When I meditate, I recapitulate the cosmic process as is consistent with my noetic code: "Yea, yea; Nay, nay." I am a macro/micro cosmic hybrid with a perspective that is introverted and extraverted, zooming in and zooming out, as fits my moment-by-moment needs and abilities.

From able Omega to needy alpha as made possible in my experience by me, the iota interface that is needy in relation to Omega and able in relation to alpha.

Lesson Fifty-Nine from My Universe to Me about Listening

Breath, drink, eat, have sex, work, and play remembering the whole Universe, Omega, behind you is being reflected uniquely by whatever alpha is in front of you. Visualize, with every breath in and out, a perfect give and take going on between you, iota, and the opposing alpha and Omega levels and sides of yourself. Your freedom and security will only be as perfect as your mindfulness of Omega first, then alpha as Omega's reflection. By putting the Omega All first, you enhance your chances of receiving the inspiration you need instantaneously.

Keep all of your plans tentative except the plan to always listen to me, Omega, first. Assume the responsibility to improve your way of relating to me and to be an example for others. The inspiration you and I share is fresh and regenerating. Keep yourself from getting hung up on false dualities. Dualistic, fixed yes or no thinking is usually stale and out of step with the times.

In order to improve your way of thinking, feeling, and acting, you must, as iota, become alpha-like enough and Omega-like enough to not be too much like either alpha or Omega relative to the needs of the moment. Hold to a vision of yourself as a dynamic and harmonious combination of all that is above and below, in back and in front, outside and inside, to the left and to the right. Your genuine value to others is in direct proportion to your understanding of how to reconcile the differences between their perspective, your perspective, and my perspective, that is, you, iota, understanding how to harmonize with alpha and Omega, each and All.

Commentary: I think it is fascinating how mindfulness meditation helps me to listen to myself and to others more carefully. It is when my mind is quiet that I can listen to reason and instinct, logic and magic, the normal world and the paranormal world, and then find the click of right balance between extremes.

I had a flat tire on my hand cycle recently, and it did not become flat until I was home. I was home instead of on the road because I had been listening to "the still small voice" within about when and how to return home. Finding my right place has been a skill that I have cultivated over many years of meditating on YyNn, the GPS code for right placement of me, iota, in relation to alpha and Omega.

I am learning how to listen first to the information that is coming in even when it is coming in as an enemy that can and sometimes does hurt me. Jesus said to agree with my adversary "quickly." I understand that phrase to mean that if we submit before reacting, listen before speaking, and relax before asserting, heaven on earth is more likely.

Lesson Sixty from My Universe to Me about Self-Mastery

In your primitive state, you were too close to nature to appreciate how special you are. In your intermediate state, you were too far from nature to appreciate how special nature is. Now, as you approach your climax state, you will balance nature and culture more and more optimally. Your mastery of nature will be secondary to your inner self-mastery. Every attempt to master nature before mastering your own inner, psychological errors will result in self-defeat. Even the apparent control you have over nature is partial and temporary.

But, once you take up the ultimate task of wisely controlling your inner life, you will temper your erroneous extremes and the natural world around you will spontaneously recover its proper balance. You have to get your own balance well-established to discover that there are no other imbalances relative to your experience of your Universe.

You are the thermostat needed to regulate the homeostatic equilibrium of the world you live in. You do this right equilibrating by wisely using yes and no to reconcile the differences of your immediate experience. As you repeat "Yea, yea; Nay, nay," the spirit of truth mantra, the comforter, while you are visualizing your tripartite model of the Self expanding and contracting optimally, you will be programming yourself to function more efficiently toward the aim of heaven on earth. Remember, when the alpha and

Omega spheres are contracting, you, the iota sphere in between, are expanding, and vice versa. Holding this optimally simplified image of your Self in mind helps you to find your way between the rocky shoal of Scylla, and the whirlpool of Charybdis, that is, between excess and deficiency.

Commentary: I lost my glasses tonight. Instead of fretting about it, I tripped my psyche's master switch with YyNn and waited for inspiration to guide me to my glasses. I soon found my glasses. How do I know that my mental discipline helped me to find my glasses? I don't, but I also do not know if such discipline did not help me find my glasses.

The advantage of having a mental discipline for solving my problems is that it makes me feel that I am the master of my experience and not the victim of it. It does not matter what happens to me, because I can use anything to make myself feel that I am gaining mastery of myself. You might say, "How do you know you are not deluding yourself?" I don't, but I also do not know that I am not the master of myself at least in some degree and maybe, because of that, an increasing degree.

Lesson Sixty-One from My Universe to Me about Self-Topology

My purpose is to teach you how to be true to me so that you in turn can teach others how to be true to me. Keep open to the learning that is optimum for you at any particular time by remembering me, Omega, first. Your "Yea, Omega" is a password to being optimally related to the each and All of your experience. Your stability, security, and survival depend on how well you order your attention. The measuring stick you need to internalize is "Yea, yea; Nay, nay," an algorithm for optimum communication between the various levels and sides of yourself.

The inspiration you need for living optimally free and secure is always available as long as you keep your mind open to me first. Relating your mind foremost to me is a skill you must master; it is putting the Whole before any part. The YyNn code that I have given you puts me first as source. It is Yea, Omega; yea, alpha; and it is Nay, alpha; nay, Omega. YyNn means that you, iota, are 1) right-receiving from me, Omega, 2) right-receiving from any alpha target; 3) right-sending to any alpha target, 4) right-sending back to Omega. It is four steps to the heaven-on-earth state of conscious balance.

This model of the Self has three nested structures and four basic functions. The structures are iota, the intermediate self between alpha, the lesser self, and Omega, the Greater Self. The functions are "Yea one, yea two; Nay one, nay two" which mean receiving, retrieving, sending, and returning respectively. Omega's functions are Nay one and yea two; alpha's functions are Yea one and nay two; iota's functions are all four, Y1, y2; N1, n2. By meditating on this model, you are cultivating an inner sense of rapport with me, Omega, helping you, iota, to solve any significant alpha problem of your experiential moment.

Commentary: You may have noticed that I do not refer to the human brain much. My experimental paradigm is based on the brain being mind-made instead of the mind being brain-made. I experience myself as a mind interfacing between my body and the world around my body. I do not experience myself as a brain.

When I died at age eleven during spinal cord surgery, I observed the flatline and the surgery crew's efforts to revive me. When I did return to life, my mind was set for life with the conviction that my life goes on after death in some form and that mind, not matter, is the maker of my life. My consciousness is fundamental to me.

The "performative contradiction" is only a contradiction to the extent that mind does not know itself. The better mind knows itself, the better it masters itself.

Lesson Sixty-Two from My Universe to Me about Life Extension

Watch out for the extremists, the oversimplifiers, the overgeneralizers, the fundamentalists, the atheists, the ageists, sexists, racists, anyone who makes too much or too little of the part or the Whole. They would do better if they knew better. You know better! You are learning how to balance well any extreme defects. You know now that you are meant to be the golden mean between all of the extremes of your experience. As iota, you are the ultimate Goldilocks figure, making the "too hot" cool enough and the "too cold" warm enough.

If you, iota, get out of balance with me, Omega, or any alpha part of me, it is your fault and you cannot blame anyone else. Your cosmos is well-proportioned only to the extent that you make it so by not distorting it with false beliefs. Step out of line with your true destiny and you get negative feedback. Learn to watch for the feedback that tells you exactly what you need to know to achieve and to maintain the meshing of our plus and minus, masculine and feminine gears.

Your conscious kingdom is built primarily from within your own mind by the way you relate your Yea one to my Nay one and your nay two to my yea two. We are designed to connect and disconnect within extremes of over-and under-connecting. Connecting well with me psychologically helps you to experience a better reflection of me physically. Enjoy meditation as our meta-sexual lovemaking, a way to have optimal life extension.

Commentary: I believe that life is a balancing act in every respect. I presuppose that the better we balance the contraries of our experience, the better we can live and the longer we can live. I have not perfected this balancing act, but I have good reasons to believe that I am getting better at it. I believe I have a noetic code that is the counterpart of the genetic code. Like the genetic code, my noetic code has four major components designed to promote more and better life.

"Yea, yea; Nay, nay" is my four-step noetic code for life improvement and life extension. The yeas are feminine and the nays are masculine. It is a hole/plug system with moving equinoctial points and resting solstitial points. When I meditate with my noetic code, I am performing meta-sexual intercourse with the each and All of my experience. It is a life-making process that I carry on with each breath in and out. The more I identify my breathing in with "Yea, yea" and out with "Nay, nay," the more I can expect my life to be improved and extended.

Practicing YyNn, as a way to prime my lower mind for optimal manifestations of my higher Mind, is my life purpose. Looking at the moon, I remember the sun.

Lesson Sixty-Three from My Universe to Me about True Destiny

Perfection is the only true quality in the Universe. Perfection is the truth about each in relation to All. Only perfection is good and beautiful; anything else is an approximation to the truth of perfection. Perfection is not perfectionism. The word perfection connotes imperfection to the mind that does not know how to think about perfection. Perfection is not sterile or tedious or tiresome or boring. If it were, it would be imperfect. Perfection is always metaphysical and never physical. Metaphysical perfection is a mental ideal that your mind needs in order to make its experience with physical phenomena as perfect as possible.

Your mind is responsible for the degree of perfection it experiences within as thoughts and feelings and outside with the objects of sense perception. You must discover by self-observation that you are the cause of the quality of experiences you have both as mental states and as physical states.

If you experiment carefully, you will find that the way to improve your experience begins by improving your thoughts. Seek the perfect standard by which you can figure out what to affirm and what to negate. Your "yes" and "no" determine how well you coincide with your true destiny. YyNn is an encrypted standard by which you can think your way into a heaven-on-earth state of conscious balance.

Commentary: I believe I have a true destiny line from which I can deviate and when I deviate too far from that true line, I get negative feedback in the form of pain and suffering. Because of my strong interest in religion and sex, I have tried to reconcile them. Most of my studies and experiments have been an effort to harmonize spirit and flesh, enhancing both without demonizing either.

In order to keep religion from being boring and sex from being shallow and meaningless, I have developed my own kind of tantric yoga. Yoes yoga is my way of finding and keeping on my true destiny line. By meditating in a way that is satisfying to my libido and uplifting to my spirit, I am able to feel well-synchronized with my true destiny; the steps I take feel better synchronized with the words I speak.

I am predestined to find, one way or another, sooner or later, the preestablished harmony that can make my world the best of all possible worlds. Currently, and for the last fifty years, my method for doing this is to contemplate "Yea, yea; Nay, nay," my default mind-set. YyNn is my "open sesame" to the kingdom of heaven on earth that I am becoming from the inside out.

Lesson Sixty-Four from My Universe to Me about True Value

Good and evil are not opposite extremes! Good is a state of being that mediates between diabolical extremes. Immature minds misinterpret the extremes and falsely conclude that one of them is always good and the other is always bad. The time has come for you to clarify the extreme ends of your experience and the way between them.

The way of true value is relative and variable and never fixed. The Absolute that I AM can be approximated well enough by the relative you. You must learn how to use your Yea One to properly match my Nay One and your nay two to properly match my yea two. Your right opening to my presenting and right presenting to my opening moderates optimally the way we are related in the here and now of your experience.

Something is of value to you because there is a place in you where it is needed. In Yoes yoga, the kind of rainbow exercise for making that happen is called a yumbow. The counterpart of a yumbow is a yabow, which is the name for the kind of rainbow exercise that helps to remove whatever is needed out of you. Fit what you need into where you need it, and you will fit where you are needed.

As your Universe, I am only as valuable as you make me. Your ongoing problem is to figure out how to keep from making too much of one side of your experience of me and too little of the other side and just enough of both sides. As you use the YyNn code to prime yourself proactively, you will find that you are entering the heaven-on-earth state of conscious balance more often.

Commentary: It was my biology studies at Oklahoma University in the 1950s that helped me to start contemplating the term *optimum* as a way past what the Bible calls "the knowledge of good and evil" that is the root of all human suffering. Plants and animals thrive when they have enough food and water; there is an optimum level, between lethal extremes, of nutrients in and waste products out that is necessary for organisms to survive. This kind of Goldilocks zone of just enough, not too much or too little, set the stage for me to graduate past the belief in a fixed "good and evil" standard of values.

About this same time in my experience I found out how nature's rainbow is made by the way an observer is positioned between sunlight from behind and a rain cloud in front. I felt liberated by the discovery of what the rainbow teaches me about the value making of the opposites of my experience; it is a problem of right alignment. Heaven on earth is a right alignment of me, iota, to any alpha part and the Omega Whole.

Lesson Sixty-Five from My Universe to Me about Paradise

Heaven and hell are a matter of here and now in your experience. Heaven is a well-balanced state of consciousness, and hell is a sense of being extremely out of balance with the each and All of your experience. YyNn is code for being well-balanced in your relationship with each and All as you experience them. Your aptitude for selecting whatever is best for you moment by moment is a kind of homeostasis that works optimally to the extent that you remember to use the YyNn code to set your mind for the golden iota point.

Work to set your mind on the iota point between the alpha and Omega extremes that are false for you. Your all-purpose set point between too much and too little, too soon and too late is the iota point, the point of Golden Section between deficiency and excess, alpha and Omega. As you persistently program yourself with "Yea, yea; Nay, nay," you develop a better feeling for the iota point.

You were programmed genetically to find the iota point of optimum balance instinctively, and then you lost the instinct for it to the extent that you became more objective and rational. Eventually you will learn how to optimally use both instinct and reason to reach the iota point in each situation you experience. Ultimately you will have both the instinct for the iota point and the understanding of it that are necessary for the refined selections required for your optimum survival. This is how paradise is given and lost and regained.

Commentary: As a child I had my own forest to play in. My friends and I ran naked through the woods, climbing trees and humping whatever was handy. It was a time of being wild and free from domestication. As I approached my teens, I was domesticated by my culture's moral code. I learned to be less selfish and more selfless, but I also felt constrained by the social rules and resisted by acting out sexually. Neither alcohol nor drugs had any interest for me. I saw them as degenerate and contrary to my fitness needs. But, sex was another thing. I sensed that sex was a necessary ingredient of my paradise.

I was raised under the influence of protestant Christians. My maternal grandmother was a saint, the most generous and hard-working person I have ever known. Her example helped to influence me to be spiritually minded. Yet, I felt that my paradise had to include sex in some form other than family making. My paradise had to be a state of being well-balanced and complete. Sex was necessary for making that happen, because paradise is essentially about making the best possible in-and-out balance the most probable in-and-out balance.

Lesson Sixty-Six from My Universe to Me about Sense Evidence

I, Omega, can help you, iota, interpret the sensory impressions you receive from the world around you in a way that will lead you to the Truth. You must realize that what you see, hear, taste, smell, and feel is not the Truth. However, you have no other way to begin your search for the Truth than that offered to you by way of your physical senses. By using your physical senses wisely, you start to free yourself from their bondage and from the false beliefs that their evidence promotes. It is important to remember that it is not the physical senses that are at fault. It is the misinformed use of these senses that results in trouble for you. It takes experience, using intuition and reason, to learn the limitations of your physical senses.

You never perceive things as they are because your means of perceiving them are always incomplete. To complete the picture, you need to develop introspection and self-observation. Turning within, you can find out how the pieces of the puzzle fit together to make a complete and well-balanced Self. Learning how to use metaphors is necessary. Your self-evolution is like a butterfly's metamorphosis. Your method of doing this is like the way an observer makes a rainbow out of raindrops and sunrays. It is an inner vision of right alignment of iota to alpha and Omega.

Your total Self, including your local self, is like a solar system with the sun representing the Greater Principle, Omega, the moon representing the lesser principle, alpha, and the earth representing the intermediate principle, iota, which is a synthesis of the Greater and the lesser principles.

The Jesus saying in the Book of Revelation: "I (iota) am alpha and Omega," is the ultimate "I am" principle for the human ego. Resist the temptation to believe that you are either one opposite or the other. You, iota, are both alpha and Omega, sometimes more one than the other, sometimes both equally but, in truth, never too much or too little of either and always enough of both.

Commentary: My universe tells me who I am when I ask to know who I am often enough and sincerely enough. As I follow my breaths in and out, I synchronize my "Yea, yea" with receiving from outside and inside and my "Nay, nay" with sending to inside and outside. As I do this, I am recapitulating the self-making process. I am a work in progress to become well-balanced and complete. My mission to be whole has resulted in being both an individual center of reference and a universal frame of reference. Physical evidence tells me about my apparent self being moonlike. Metaphysical evidence tells me about my real Self being sunlike.

Lesson Sixty-Seven from My Universe to Me about Dialectical Optimism

First you segregate yourself, and then you integrate yourself. Your psychological development involves a process of separating yourself from the mass-mindedness of undeveloped humanity. It can only be done by a conscious effort to understand who you are and how you are distinct from the rest of mankind. Eventually, after you have gained enough insight, you come back to earth psychologically and admit to yourself how valuable others are to you and how helpless you are without them.

Your assignment is to individualize me, your Universe, in a way that is valuable to others in their efforts to individualize their Universe. The people most helpful to your development are the ones who are most sincere in their efforts to be whole. They exemplify the vigilant effort it takes to avoid diabolical dualism by practicing dialectical optimism. It is easy to be a specialist who loses touch with the ecological and holistic nature of reality or to be one who overgeneralizes and loses touch with the special needs of a particular situation.

How can you find and keep the balance that is optimum for you? First, you must realize that optimum balance is dynamic; it is not something that can be fixed once and forever. However, you can learn the meditation method I am teaching you to optimally equilibrate the various levels and sides of yourself. It is a method of inner self-communication based on the encrypted statement at Matthew 5:37: "Let your communication be Yea, yea; Nay, nay."

Commentary: YyNn is the code that my Self-Designed Universe gave me to use for intelligent self-design. Like produces like, and the greater controls the lesser to the extent that the intermediate, iota, lets the greater, Omega, control the lesser, alpha, in iota's experience of alpha. As iota, I am the dialectical synthesis of an alpha antithesis to my Omega thesis. Using YyNn as a meditation technique, I oscillate between my Omega's too much and too little, and my alpha's too little and too much to make an ideal synthesis of just right.

Using sets and reps of YyNn, I am communicating with my alpha mind, who lives on the quality of light that I share with her and reproduces in accord with that quality of light. If I send her distortions of my Omega mind's light, she reproduces those distortions. As I envision the perfection of my Omega mind's light, using YyNn, alpha reproduces more of that right light, in concrete terms, for me to enjoy in my everyday experience.

Lesson Sixty-Eight from My Universe to Me about Survival

The time has come for you to juggle the various sides of your experience in a new way, a way based on the YyNn code for optimum inner self-communication. The irregular and sometimes chaotic stages leading up to your present stage of development have been necessary preparation for the refinement that is coming your way. Your optimum survival depends on your readiness.

Only a select kind of human consciousness will qualify for survival. You will qualify if you use well the leads I give you. I will lead you to climax consciousness, the ultimate balancing act, the purpose for all of the conflict that has been leading up to the final stabilization of challenge and growth.

The climax stage of consciousness development can be attained by you, the Universe individualized. It has been attained by others. It is only now becoming possible and necessary for a collective climax to be reached in your world of experience.

If this climax in human consciousness is reached in time, the experiment of life on earth will have served its true purpose. I am leading you but you must make right and timely requests of me in order to receive my leads. The only way you can help anyone else to quality for optimum survival is to let me help you first. Prepare a place for me in your heart and keep it ready for my leads by meditating on "Yea, yea; Nay, nay," the ultimate, all-purpose, survival mantra.

Commentary: You realize by now of course that I am making one presupposition after another without giving you much evidence to confirm what I am presupposing. Most of what I have been experiencing for the last seventy years has been confirmation enough for me that I am on the right course, the course that is approximating ever more closely to what I like to call heaven on earth.

The heaven-on-earth state of conscious balance is a climax state that I am designing with the YyNn algorithm. YyNn is four mind-setting steps that I have turned into an exercise system. I call the mind/body exercise system, based on YyNn, rainbow making, the ritual of general practice of Yoes yoga. I teach my yoga, based on YyNn, to individuals who select me to do so. Our learning and teaching is a process of mutual selection that either of us can take or leave as our inspiration moves us. I am a YyNn decoder; I am not an authority on anything but the YyNn quality control of my own conscious experience.

Lesson Sixty-Nine from My Universe to Me about Peace

The war between opposing differences will not be won by a national government. It is won by you or any individual who figures out how to harmonize the alpha and Omega principles of their own psyche. The concept of good and evil as fixed white and black values is the cause of all extreme human error.

A rainbow bridge must be made between the basic kinds of opposing extremes within you that light and darkness symbolize in the world of material appearances. If you win the war inside, you cannot lose the war outside. You must realize that the primary battle field is within you. You are responsible for using yes and no in ways that reconcile the alpha and Omega sides and levels of yourself. Resist the belief that one side of your world of experience must ultimately win over the other side.

Peace will never come to your world as long as you believe that peace is a result of one side finally winning and the other side finally losing. Peace must be understood and demonstrated as a dynamic process of ongoing modification of contrasting extremes. You, as a conscious individual, are between these experiential extremes, and you must learn how to use one extreme to optimally moderate the other extreme, self-correcting in line with your true destiny. To do this well enough and often enough is to live an optimum kind of war and peace.

Mediocrity is a moderate deviation from optimum moderation. Tragedy is an extreme deviation from optimum moderation. Health is an optimum moderation of lethal extremes. Excellence is an optimum moderation of the sterile and the tacky. True goodness and beauty are not extremes—they are golden means between false extremes.

Commentary: Contemplation on and meditation with YyNn is the backbone of my personal journey. I began meditating at the age of eleven when I had an out-of-body experience during spinal cord surgery at the Mayo Clinic in 1946. As I watched my body die, I was awakened to the possibility of finding a way to live that was more dependent on my mind than my body. I found a chance to have peace within by taking command of my mind-set. Eventually I found the "Yea, yea; Nay, nay" mantra and knew the way to a heaven-on-earth mind-set was mine to cultivate and possibly mine to master and to demonstrate for the benefit of anyone willing to do the work required.

Lesson Seventy from My Universe to Me about the Golden Mean

You have the endless responsibility of creating and reconciling differences optimally. You are tempted at every turn to make too much or too little out of each or All. The diabolically dualistic domain of error is sliced truthfully by the narrow path you are designed to take step by step from here to eternity. Each step you take will be as truthful as your understanding and watchfulness make possible. If you want harmony more than discord, wisdom more than ignorance, you must be willing to pay attention to what makes each moment of your experience a solution to the yes-or-no decision problem.

Watch your thoughts, feelings, and actions and bring them into accord with what is encoded as: "Yea, yea; Nay, nay." It is a vision of the Golden Rule as a way you can reach and maintain the golden mean. It is a vision of the Golden Rule that has iota, the conscious individual, doing right by both the alpha part and the Omega Whole, thereby producing a dynamic state of golden meaning.

You make a psychological rainbow when you, iota, remember the truth about yourself as alpha and Omega harmonized. The deep and golden meaning of the Golden Rule is a form of practicable magic. Replace the diabolical worldview with the ecological and dialectical worldview, and you will stand a better chance of achieving the wisdom and harmony that is true for you, a golden mean between extravagance and poverty. Oscillate optimally between the alpha and Omega extremes as the golden iota who knows how to make the rainbow effect everywhere and forever.

Commentary: Aristotle said courage is the golden mean between rashness and cowardice. I like to extend that idea to all of my human experience and see that I am a potential self-made, golden synthesis of all of the so called opposites. That means that my potential is feminine and masculine, young and old, needy and able, liberal and conservative, and dark and light. However, my problem is to figure out how to optimally balance the opposites of my potential and to not get stuck in being too much or too little of either kind of opposite and enough of both kind of opposite here and now.

"Yea, yea; Nay, nay" is the basis of a meditation system that I consciously use to prime my adaptive unconscious mind for optimum balance of the too much and too little, too soon and too late opposites of my experience. Does it work? Let me show you how to try it; you will be amazed if you are one of the elect called to it.

Afterword

My entire experience of seventy-six years so far has been mainly about learning how to regulate my inner life in a way that makes my outer life better. After learning from others about inner self-improvement, I set out to make my own self-making system. This book was designed to help me become better at explaining my system of spiritual practices and to help you find information that might be useful in your efforts to make your own system of personal inner practice.

I think I am putting together something that might eventually become the yoga that Carl Jung predicted would "be laid down on the basis of Christianity." My system is an inner, esoteric kind of Christianity—not the exoteric traditional Christianity. It is a system of metaphysical exercises to be synchronized with physical exercises. I have not explained these exercises in much detail in this book because I prefer to do that on a person-by-person, customized basis. I teach my meditation system to individuals who feel called to try it out.

It is not important to me that anyone wanting to experiment with my way of meditating be on the same page with me about anything except the possibility that "Yea, yea; Nay, nay" is the "open sesame" to the human subconscious mind's capacity to manifest a well-balanced, heaven-on-earth state of conscious, human experience. I have noticed, as my inner life is getting more harmonious, it matters less how my outer life shapes up. For example, I use to think that walking free again would be what would make me happiest, but now I know that it is winning the inner game of life that makes me happiest.

The secret is not getting the universe to do my will; it is to get myself into sync with the will of the Universe as it applies to me. How do I know when I am in sync with the will of the Universe as it applies to me? I do not know that, but I do know that is my intention, because I meditate night and day on that right intention encoded as "Yea, yea; Nay, nay."

I hope this book helps you to know if you want to learn more about my interpretation and application of "Yea, yea; Nay, nay" as four steps to the heaven-on-earth state of conscious balance.

Appendix One

Affirmations and Comments Based on the Decoding of
"Yea, yea; Nay, nay" and "I am alpha and Omega"

1. I am alpha and Omega uniquely synthesized as iota.

2. I am alpha and Omega harmonized by being sometimes
   more like alpha than Omega and sometimes more like
   Omega than alpha and sometimes equally like both alpha
   and Omega, and in truth, never too much or too little like
   either and always enough like both.

3. As iota, I am a perfect synthesis of alpha and Omega
   attributes.

4. As rainbows are made by a right alignment of an observer
   with sunrays and raindrops, so I, as iota, make rainbowlike
   relationships out of the alpha and Omega contraries of my
   personal experience.

5. I am an optimal blend of alpha's receptivity and Omega's
   potency.

6. The yin and yang of my experience correspond to the alpha
   and Omega principles of the YyNn code; the Tao of my
   experience corresponds to a proper balance of my yin and
   yang, alpha and Omega principles, by means of my conscious
   choices as iota.

7. I am the heaven-on-earth state of balance when I am conscious of myself as alpha and Omega equilibrated optimally in my here and now.

8. My consciousness as iota creates a better body and world for me to the extent that I become the servant of Omega and the master of alpha.

9. Omega is my master and alpha is my servant; alpha loves and serves me to the extent that I love and serve Omega.

10. As iota, I am impregnated by the absolute Truth from Omega, and in turn, I impregnate alpha with that Truth to get concrete evidence of relative truth reflected in my everyday experience.

11. As iota, I set my mind with YyNn, the template for the heaven-on-earth state of balance.

12. Omega is my super mind-set, alpha is any sub mind-set of Omega that I, iota, focus on. I emerge from an alpha to become more like Omega until I am enough like Omega to be of help to any particular alpha.

13. I am alpha and Omega, yielding and firm, shy and bold, feminine and masculine, young and old, Dionysus and Apollo, Charybdis and Scylla. "Yea, yea; Nay, nay" is the code by which I, iota, can make a true, here-and-now balance out of any of these extremes.

14. I set my mind with "Yea, yea; Nay, nay" in order to condition myself for an optimum distribution of the conservative and the liberal, self-serving and self-sacrificing, sometimes more one than the other, sometimes equally both, but never too much or too little of either and always enough of both.

15. In Yoes meditation, I send light that I love to others so they have the light they need to love. Because I love the light Omega sends to me, alpha loves the light I send to her. Omega is the primary light sender/retriever; alpha is the primary light receiver/reflector; iota, in the middle, is both a light receiver/reflector and a light sender/retriever. YyNn is code for the optimum circulation of light waves from Omega to iota and light particles from iota to alpha and light particles from alpha to iota and light waves from iota to Omega and back again.

16. I am tempted to think that people are what they are in my experience because that is simply what they are regardless of what I am as an observer. However, that is a naïve way to think, because I affect the way they are in my experience by the mind-set I bring to my experience of them. The rainbow-making mind-set, YyNn, is designed to help me remember the Omega All, so I will see others reflecting Omega in my experience in just the way they need to for my benefit and theirs. This is how to practice the rainbow-making effect of the saying, "what blesses one blesses all."

17. My "I am" is your "I am" to the extent that you find it useful as a way to identify and optimize yourself as alpha and Omega, the each and All of your experience. My YyNn mojo can become your YyNn mojo if you want it to.

18. "Yea, yea; Nay, nay" is a template for setting iota, the self-conscious human mind, for the best possible relationship with the Omega Whole and any alpha part of that Omega Whole. My iota mind is set with YyNn for hanging on and letting go optimally to alpha and Omega, enough of both and not too much or too little of either.

19. Yes, I am presupposing that humans now are to be made obsolete if they do not change within. Mother Nature, generic alpha, is good at making organisms that serve as stepping stones to better-adapted organisms. It is a dialectical pattern of organisms challenged by environment resulting in organisms better-adapted to that environment. Humans are creating the very environment that will eliminate them if they do not change within, and I presuppose that change must come from within as more mind-controlling matter and less matter-controlling mind. I also am presupposing, for the sake of experimentation, that YyNn is code for the change within needed for my evolution and for human evolution in general. YyNn is a communication code, a self-communication code that Jesus, or someone using the name of Jesus, gave me to improve my communication with myself for the purposes of adapting better to my environment and meeting the needs for myself and others to thrive using YyNn.

20. Concessions to the belief that we are matter-made instead of mind-made are necessary until we reach the point in our climb where we are ready to claim our freedom step by step, thought by thought, out of matter into mind, out of the belief we are matter-made into the understanding that we are mind-made. Reaching that point is the *mu* point in the alpha to Omega self-spectrum of the YyNn code. It is just before *nu,* where the light of Omega Mind reaches iota mind directly instead of only indirectly via alpha mind. Then the rest of the mental climb becomes clearer as to where and how we are going, but not easier. The higher we get, the harder the climb, but we are stronger for making it to where we are. We finally escape the pull of alpha mind's gravity, and then we can circulate in our own well-earned heavenly mental orbit, optimally poised between heaven and earth principles, sometimes closer to one than the other, sometimes equal distant from both, but never too far from or too close to either and always far enough from and close enough to both.

21. The basic Yoes code mantra is: Yea, Omega/yea, alpha/Nay, alpha/nay, Omega!

22. The Yoes code equation for self identification and self optimization is: Iota (YyNn) = alpha (Yn) + Omega (Ny).

Appendix Two

Definitions of Rainbow Making

1. Rainbow making (RM) is the ritual of the general practice of Yoes code.

2. RM is a combination of the best from ancient religion and modern science.

3. RM is a coherent theory and practice for explaining and demonstrating the truth about one's self.

4. RM is based on a concept of one's self as a trinity in unity overcoming duality.

5. RM is a technique for harmonizing human thought, feeling, speech, and action.

6. RM is a way to make one's life a lovemaking experience.

7. RM is the reconciliation of opposites.

8. RM is the equilibration of extremes.

9. RM is levitation and gravitation utilized for optimization.

10. RM is relating one's body to the world in a way that is a help to both and harmful to neither.

11. RM is a way of meditating on perfection that is self-gratifying and self-renewing.

12. RM is consciousness creating a better body by transcending sense impressions to the contrary.

13. RM makes more out of approximations to the good, true, and beautiful and less out of deviations from the good, true, and beautiful.

14. RM is the dynamic equilibrium called homeostasis that every healthy organism achieves but that only the conscious human organism can learn to sustain.

15. RM is a way of achieving the golden mean by practicing the Golden Rule.

16. RM is a help to the human mind in figuring out how to keep from over-and under-simplifying everything.

17. RM is fire and water, optimally combined and distributed.

18. RM makes it possible for ego, super-ego, and id to live together in harmony.

19. RM is an ecological way of living that reconciles evolution and special creation, natural selection and intelligent design.

20. RM bridges the gap of ignorance created by the passing of each moment with faith that the information needed each moment is always available.

21. RM is a psychosomatic exercise system founded on a unified field theory of the Self.

22. RM is both fun and serious but neither supercilious nor grave.

23. RM is a way the human mind can figure out itself by learning how to interpret the language of nature.

24. RM can be taught well by someone who knows how to use "Yea, yea; Nay, nay" to make the optimally balanced state called the iota point, the point of Golden Section as applied to human experience.

25. RM is meditation on the life process as a lovemaking process.

26. RM is a therapy for the human ego, helping it to achieve and maintain the most precarious of balancing acts.

27. RM is the ultimate and the intimate combined as the optimate.

28. RM is the conscious human mind deprogramming the subconscious human mind of error and reprogramming it with truth in order to have optimal personal survival.

29. RM is meditation brought down to earth in a way that makes heaven on earth possible.

30. RM is going on anytime a relationship is helpful to both and harmful to neither.

31. RM is supply and demand, well-arranged for each and All.

32. RM is reaping whatever is best in order to sow whatever is best.

33. RM is making ends meet and unmeet wisely.

34. RM is inspirational and practical, the art/science of living well.

35. RM is pure alpha and pure Omega self-reproducing as a vigorous hybrid named iota.

36. RM is a way of mixing business and pleasure that enhances both and denigrates neither.

37. RM is the true and narrow way home without succumbing to the rocks of Scylla (excess) or to the whirlpool of Charybdis (deficiency).

38. RM is a system of holistic exercises, some of which are called sunbows, moonbows, and earthbows. There are three kinds earthbows: *yumbows, yobows,* and *yabows.*

39. RM uses the human hand as a cosmological handbook with the fist, open hand, and each finger being symbolic of basic life principles.

40. RM helps the human mind not to make itself up prematurely or post-maturely.

41. RM teaches one how to stop thinking too much in terms of either/or and how to start thinking more in terms of both/and—a change that is essential to the survival of life on earth.

42. RM teaches an absolute that is All and a relative opposite that is each, and an intermediate combination of these opposites that is both All and each, eternal and temporal, infinite and finite, objective and subjective, absolute and relative.

43. RM determines values within the experiential here and now instead of according to a fixed tradition or dogma.

44. RM is breathing in and breathing out in a way that reminds one of the nourishing and purifying phases of life's cycles, a recapitulation of the cosmic process encoded as "Yea, yea; Nay, nay."

45. RM is an inner-work system that makes life work well and look like a rainbow instead of a gapbow or jambow.

46. RM is a collaboration of the masculine and feminine principles in a way that results in the androgynous principle: Iota (YyNn) = alpha (Yn) + Omega (Ny).

47. RM is consistent with the pattern of the Golden Section and shows the practical application of this pattern as a meditation technique.

48. RM uses yes and no to establish optimal boundaries symbolized by the word *Yoes*.

49. RM is a psychosomatic technology for identifying and optimizing oneself based on the Yoes code: "Yea, yea; Nay, nay."

50. RM helps one to be in the place he or she needs to be to reap and sow optimally.

51. RM is a method of oscillating optimally between all that is above and below, behind and in front, outside and inside, to the left and to the right.

52. RM is so called because it makes the RM practitioner a beautiful state of being, which, like the rainbow, results from a strategic angle of relatedness of observer to the arch antipodes: fire (masculinity) and water (femininity).

53. RM teaches that the optimum angle of relatedness of self to each and All is what is always needed and what is always available.

54. RM is holistic health, a personal state poised within the extremes of too much and too little, too soon and too late.

55. RM is a kind of mind-over-matter self-imaging that challenges the so-called "performative contradiction."

56. RM is freedom and order, spontaneity and planning, letting go and hanging on, yielding and standing firm, receptivity and potency experienced in golden proportions.

57. RM makes compatibles out of spirit and nature and shows how the one is helpless without the other; spirit needs to be grounded in nature and nature needs to be uplifted by spirit.

58. RM produces rainbow warriors, the agents of defense for the body and the planet.

59. RM produces an optimum balance of loving and fighting, accepting and rejecting, attracting and repelling, faith and doubt, yes and no.

60. RM demonstrates the intelligence needed to make choices and experience changes that optimize personal and social stability, security and survival.

61. RM helps one learn how to behave in a way that is ecologically fit and consistent with the next step in human evolution.

62. RM is a software program for the human, adaptive unconscious that makes it possible for the contraries of

personal experience to collaborate in making the butterfly stage of human evolution.

63. RM turns enemies into friends by making the too much less enough and the too little more enough, encoded as YyNn, the sex-act pattern behind all of creation.

64. RM is the process whereby reason moderates desire and desire enlivens reason, enough of both and not too much of either relative to immediate experience.

65. RM is possibly destined to become a fad that will help make maturity possible for the human race.

66. RM is a way of playing the game of life that makes it possible for iota, the intermediate principle, to win and lose optimally in relation to alpha, the lesser principle, and Omega, the greater principle.

67. RM postulates that mediocrity is a moderate deviation from perfect moderation and tragedy is an extreme deviation from perfect moderation.

68. RM is the YyNn understanding that makes it possible to demonstrate the concordant coincidence of iota with alpha and Omega.

69. RM is the covert rehearsing of the Paragon model of the Self, encoded as YyNn.

70. RM is a style of life that manages stress optimally by bringing thought, feeling, and action into obedience to the YyNn rules of the true road.

Appendix Three

Rainbow Making Exercises Based on the Morning Star Mandala

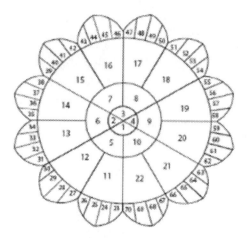

1) Yumbow
2) Yobow
3) Yabow
4) Yobow

5) Yumbow
6) Yobow
7) Yabow
8) Yabow
9) Yobow
10) Yumbow

11) Yumbow
12) Yumbow
13) Yobow
14) Yobow
15) Yobow
16) Yobow
17) Yobow
18) Yobow
19) Yobow
20) Yobow
21) Yumbow
22) Yumbow

23) Yumbow
24) Yumbow
25) Yumbow
26) Yumbow
27) Yumbow
28) Yumbow
29) Yumbow
30) Yumbow
31) Yobow

32) Yobow
33) Yobow
34) Yobow
35) Yobow
36) Yobow
37) Yobow
38) Yobow
39) Yobow
40) Yabow
41) Yabow
42) Yabow
43) Yabow
44) Yabow
45) Yabow
46) Yabow
47) Yabow
48) Yabow
49) Yabow
50) Yabow
51) Yabow
52) Yabow
53) Yabow
54) Yabow
55) Yobow
56) Yobow
57) Yobow
58) Yobow
59) Yobow
60) Yobow
61) Yobow
62) Yobow
63) Yobow
64) Yumbow
65) Yumbow
66) Yumbow
67) Yumbow
68) Yumbow
69) Yumbow
70) Yumbow

Appendix Four

Music of the Spheres

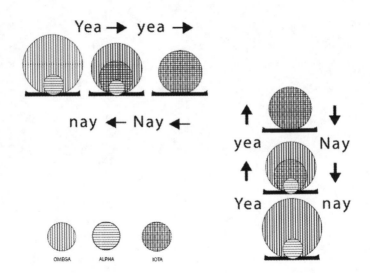